THE JUNIOR DEAN

The Junior Dean
RB McDowell

ENCOUNTERS WITH A LEGEND

Edited by

Anne Leonard

THE LILLIPUT PRESS
DUBLIN

First published 2003 by
THE LILLIPUT PRESS LTD
62–63 Sitric Road, Arbour Hill,
Dublin 7, Ireland
www.lilliputpress.ie

A CIP record for this title is available from
The British Library.

1 3 5 7 9 10 8 6 4 2

ISBN 1 84351 038 3

Set in 11 on 13pt Sabon
Design: SUSAN WAINE

Printed in Ireland by ßetaprint, Clonshaugh, Dublin

FRONTISPIECE:
RB McDowell leaving the Rubrics by Derek Hill
by courtesy of the Executors of the Estate

Contents

ACKNOWLEDGMENTS

I would like to thank all of the alumni and friends who sent their reminiscences, anecdotes and tall stories to create this book and to the chairmen of the various Associations who passed my requests for material to members.

In College, the following individuals and bodies were especially helpful: The Provost, Dr John Hegarty; Dr Paula Murphy, Assistant Junior Dean; Professor Brendan Kennelly; Dr RA Somerville; Dr WE Vaughan; Brendan Tangley, Junior Dean; Brendan Dempsey, Audio Visual & Media Service (Photography) TCD; Brian McGovern, Audio Visual & Media Service (Photography) TCD; Ian Boyle, Editor of *Trinity News* 2002/3; Renata McDonnell, Editor *Trinity News* 2003/4; Trinity Foundation; Michael Gleeson, Secretary to the College and Monica Alcock; Norah Kelso, Alumni Association Office.

I am grateful to The Publications Committee, for its kind permission to print extracts and photographs from *Trinity News* and *TCD, A College Miscellany*; to the Executors of Derek Hill's Estate, for permission to reproduce 'RB McDowell leaving the Rubrics'; to Rosalind Mulholland, for her watercolour, 'Dr McDowell in the Long Room' and to the Audio Visual & Media Service (Photography) TCD, for permission to print sketches of College in the 1950s by Bryan de Grineau. Thanks are also due to The Random Press Group Ltd, for its permission to print an extract from *A Moveable Feast* by Ernest Hemingway.

Others who have been especially helpful are Pauline Millington-Ward and Alan Cook.

Thank you in anticipation to all those who have stories up their sleeves but are still thinking about sending them in. Perhaps these may contribute to a later volume, for there is no doubt that many more 'McDowell stories' are still out there, awaiting the imprint of pen on paper.

And finally, all of my thanks to Dr McDowell – the inspiration for this book and all of the stories in it – who has so enlivened the narrative with his own memories and apposite comments.

Introduction

Two events, separated by almost ten years, provided the impetus for this book. The first was Dr McDowell's 80th birthday party at the Boat Club in London. People say that there were six, eight and even twelve of these celebrations, but this was the most famous. The Boathouse was packed and featured an enormous cake bearing the world-famous insignia of hat and keys; amazing tales were told, all starring the JD, after which he stood up and told even better ones, all about himself. A great occasion! I remember thinking that these anecdotes should go into a book before they were forgotten, for 'McDowell Stories' are always enjoyable and people love to hear them.

But nothing more happened until, nearly ten years later, I went to a TCD luncheon in Cambridge. By now, it was July 2002. The Speaker, a Fellow of St John's College, spoke of the reciprocal arrangements that have existed between Trinity and St John's for the past few centuries, adding that when he first arrived, he learned that the previous occupant of his rooms had been an unusual gentleman from Trinity College, Dublin, called Dr RB McDowell. At once, the audience sat up and buzzed a bit, hoping for some RB stories. They were not disappointed. The Speaker told a few untrue anecdotes but that didn't matter to appreciative applause and then members of the audience joined in and told more of their own. Just one week later – over at Selwyn College – another luncheon, another speaker and more stories and at that point I thought, 'That's it! Something must be done!'

So I went home and wrote to the Associations and as many miscreants as I could remember, saying: 'Now that we are hurtling
towards Dr McDowell's 90th birthday, I would like to collect all of
those myths and legends that have kept us so entertained over the
years, and would hope to publish a small book in time for the event.
Please send your own favourite stories soonest, etc.' All over the
world, Alumni set to work. Seizing pen, pencil, typewriter and com-
puter, they wrote down their memories, anecdotes, stories old and
new, tall tales and adventures, dispatching all of them by post, fax,
email, courier and telephone. The results of their labours were div-
erse, humorous and numerous.

There was only one flaw: when Dr McDowell saw certain famous
tales about himself, he said they just were not true, even 'off-beam!'
and, indeed, accounts of the same incident do often differ, embellished by time and an understandable wish to impress one's listener.
However, the variant versions have been included here so that, aided
by an occasional astute comment from Dr McDowell himself, readers
may decide for themselves to what extent absolute truth is required
for the enjoyment of a good story. Please read on!

ANNE LEONARD
London, 31 August 2003

TRIBUTES TO DR RB McDOWELL

'A luminary of a vanishing Ireland and a vanishing Academe.
May he continue for a long time to light our way.'
LORD MOYNE

'Over the years, when I have been mostly either in Ireland or America,
McDowell has been mostly in London, so our paths have seldom
crossed, although always to our mutual gratification when the
crossing happened. We have also reviewed one another's books,
almost always favourably.
So best wishes to the Junior Dean on his 90th birthday!
Hoping to see him soon.'
DR CONOR CRUISE O'BRIEN

'A Man of Great Spirit,
a Talker in the Tradition of Oscar Wilde,
a Superb Writer and Scholar.'
PROFESSOR BRENDAN KENNELLY

DR RB McDOWELL
Professor, Emeritus Fellow and Junior Dean of Trinity College, Dublin
PHOTO: BRYAN McGOVERN

In the Beginning

A MOVEABLE FEAST

In 1592 Queen Elizabeth I granted a charter for a university in Ireland and Trinity College was built 'juxta Dublin' on the site of All Hallows, a former Augustinian priory. By the eighteenth century Trinity was being called the 'University of the Protestant Ascendancy'; in 1793 Catholics were admitted; women undergraduates arrived in 1904; ex-servicemen added a mature presence in the 1940s, and by the 1950s and 1960s the intake was very international. Almost 40 per cent of undergraduates came from the UK, 40 per cent from Eire and approximately 20 per cent from other countries, notably the USA, Canada, Australia, India, Pakistan and Europe – a cosmopolitan backdrop against which most of the following stories took place.

By the 1950s Dr McDowell had become famous. He appeared regularly on radio and television and, as a renowned wit, was reputed to spend his weekends as a guest in the great houses of Ireland. He featured regularly in the College and Dublin press, and on being appointed Junior Dean, with his new disciplinary profile and frequent appearances at all the major social events in College, he quickly became a legend.

Given the relatively small number of undergraduates at that time – about two thousand – and the residential atmosphere of College, people felt that they were in, and belonged to, a very special place indeed. It is a feeling that you never lose, no matter how long you have been away. As Ernest Hemingway said of Paris:

'If you are lucky enough to have lived in Paris as a young man, then wherever you go for the rest of your life, it stays with you, for Paris is a moveable feast.'

Trinity was our moveable feast and Dr RB McDowell became its symbol.

'THE GOLDEN ERA'

Years after leaving College and having (I thought) forgotten all this, I went to a party in Pimlico. On arrival, my host called down the stairs: 'There's a surprise for you here at the top!' Well, there was a surprise at the bottom for on the banisters lay a hat, coat and scarf that you couldn't forget, ever! And then I heard the voice. As Henry Clark says later in this book, 'You couldn't miss it in a crowd of a million!' The voice emanated from the drawing-room wherein stood Dr McDowell, looking just the same, holding forth to a group of amazed girls. He didn't pause for breath: 'Ah,' said he, 'Anne Leonard! – last of the Golden Era!' This was the first I had heard of a 'Golden Era' but I liked the sound of it and was pleased to hear that I had been in it. Afterwards, I wondered what it was and when it had taken place and realized that 'The Golden Era' meant 'The Era of McDowell', for he has been an integral part of Trinity for seventy-one years now – almost one sixth of the entire life of the university. This 'Era', therefore, began in 1932, the year in which RB McDowell entered College. It was a different world! A.L.

1930S

In the early thirties I was invited to a dance at The Provost's House, Trinity College, Dublin, given by the then Provost, Edward Gwyn. It was, and is, one of the finest houses in Ireland and this was a most brilliant event. On arrival, we were presented with programmes to which were attached tiny pencils. The staircase was seen to full advantage as we made our way to be presented to the Gwyn family. This was a most memorable evening. I was fortunate to have F. La Touche Godfrey as my tutor. He was very understanding and always ready to help. Other lecturers who made their subjects so interesting were Professor Curtis, Professor Constantia Maxwell and Professor Rudmoss-Brown, just to mention a few.

Another wonderful memory that I have of my time at Trinity was when I was selected as one of the members of the tennis team to tour the English universities in the early thirties. It was arranged that we would play Oxford, Cambridge, Bedford, Birmingham and London. For some reason, Cambridge had to cancel. The entire tour lasted approximately ten days and was the greatest success and as a result I got my colours. Then, about seventy-two years later, I learnt that I was entitled to a 'Trinity Pink', which had only recently become available to all women who had been awarded their colours.

OLIVE CARROLL-LEAHY (MacDONALD) (1936)

DR McDOWELL WRITES:

The following may prove a useful background. I was born in September 1913 and was educated at RBAI and Trinity College, Dublin. I entered TCD in 1932, graduated BA in 1936 and PhD in 1938. Then, after being engaged in a variety of occupations including librarianship, school-mastering and deputy lecturing, I was appointed a lecturer in Trinity in 1945, elected a Fellow in 1951 and held the post of Junior Dean from 1956 to 1969. Much of my time was spent in reading and writing. Reading proved to be both intellectually enriching and self-indulgent – I read strenuously, but also for amusement, for instance, a quantity of novels. As for writing, I sometimes found it enjoyable, though often it was against the grain.

1940S

I went up to Trinity in 1946 and got to know RB quite early in my first year. He was an only son, his family coming originally from Derry, and I seem to remember that his father, who had been a tea merchant, was dead before I knew RB. He grew up, however, in Belfast and went to 'Inst.' or RBAI and his mother lived in Belfast until she died in about 1960 – I met her once, a very pleasant Malone Road matron. RB used to go up to Belfast fairly regularly to see her.

Joint 21st party – Robin Tamplin and Henry Clark – at The Boat Club, November 1949. *Left to right*: Dr Norman Furlong, H. Clark, Tom Moir (PhD student from the USA), Mrs Moir and RB. *Foreground*: Christy Byrne, boatman.

From Inst. RB came to Trinity, got 'Scol' and a good Mod. in History in 1935 or 1936 (he has no entry in *Who's Who*, so one cannot check, nor is he in that dreary book, *Modern Irish Lives*). His first job was as Librarian of the ancient Marsh's Library near St Patrick's for two or three years I guess, a job that gave him a little prestige as a scholar and time and opportunity for historical research.

When the war came, RB went to England and, as his war work, became a temporary master at Radley, replacing someone who had joined the Forces. He was at that time inevitably well-known by sight to Radleans and he made life-long friends with Oliver Sutchbury and his brother. S.P.B. Mais, quite a distinguished pre-war writer, was also a temporary schoolmaster at Radley and, I'm told, spoke highly of RB's prose style! I met the Sutchbury brothers at RB's 60th birthday – a dinner he gave a few of us at the Reform Club. Both of them worked in the City as bankers but will have retired by now.

It wasn't until after the War in 1945 or '46 that RB came back to Trinity as a lecturer (I think). I was probably the first of the less academic sort of student who asked RB to parties in my rooms and to the Trial VIII dinners at the Boat Club, etc. But very soon he became a familiar sight at student parties and was very well-liked. He also became well-known at Hist debates – he may, I think, have won a Hist gold medal in oratory as a student and was certainly an Honorary Member, though he hadn't been Auditor.

HENRY CLARK (1950)

The Junior Dean crossing Front Square, 1966 (see page 62)

PHOTO: CHRIS JOHNSTON

Junior Dean

1956 – 1969

APPOINTMENT

*I*n *1956, Dr RB McDowell was appointed Junior Dean and at first his contemporaries were amazed, for he was an unexpected choice. They soon saw, however, that the job was made for him, thanks to his remarkable ability to blend discipline with friendship, which he did with a verve and a dash never seen before – or since – and he took to his new role like a duck to water. People realized that his appointment was not so much surprising as inspired and he was to remain Junior Dean for thirteen years, the longest-ever holder of the appointment.* A.L.

He was the most popular and successful Junior Dean in living memory. R. DESMOND LEWIS (1944)

McDowell became Junior Dean and was responsible for discipline on the campus. Misled by certain eccentricities of manner, some undergraduates 'tried it on', expecting to get away with it. They soon found out their mistake. McDowell was effortlessly and effectively tough as a disciplinarian, where discipline was required, while otherwise being unfailingly helpful to the majority of undergraduates who behaved themselves appropriately.
DR CONOR CRUISE O'BRIEN (1940)

The best thing that happened to RB was to be elected a Fellow in 1951 and to become Junior Dean in 1956, which meant that he moved to rooms in the Rubrics. He gave a new character to the post and performed it very well. He knew the students better than any of the faculty or Fellows and was liked by of all the students and by the porters who worked for him. He was the best Junior Dean since Bobby Tait in the 1920s! His immediate predecessor, Frank Mitchell, had been a very dry stick, though a good biologist and naturalist. A lot of people who were at Trinity in the 1950s to this day just call RB, 'the JD'. HENRY CLARK (1950)

When Dr McDowell was appointed JD, some of the students decided to celebrate his new position and his removal to his new rooms. On the appointed day, there was major confusion in Front Square, as two enormous pantechnicons – with trailers – arrived in the Square and tried to back into the North Side. One of the men went in to size up the situation and shouted back to his colleague, 'For Jaysus sake, what we need here is a f...ing dustbin!' With that, three American-made taxis arrived to transport RB McD himself. Quite unfazed by all of this, he came up to me and said, 'Webb, I am going up to the University Club and the only transport I'm expecting today is the delivery of a bag of coal.' CHARLIE WEBB-PORTER (1957)

I remember our astonishment when he was appointed Junior Dean, only to learn how few flies were on him when he went into action! DR KATHLEEN WELLS (MacLARNON) (1950)

When *Trinity News* started, I both wrote and drew pictures for it. When Dr McD was elected Junior Dean, there is (if any of the first back numbers still exist) a picture of him as a Spanish fighting-bull with his own face and the caption, '*Olé, Novillo!*' I had just returned from a month in Spain and I thought my caption to be very clever, but I now realize that the drawing was second-rate and the writing juvenile. DR HENRY SMITH (1957)

As Junior Dean he is efficient and popular, though the extent to which his amazing secretary, Mrs Crawford, is responsible for the first, is difficult to tell. He has a frightening knowledge of the goings-on in College. When he acts, he is firm, if a little excited and flustered. RB McDowell is obsessed with both being and appearing fair. His predecessor as JD ruled in military style and few students desired to live in College. Judged by these standards, McDowell's reign is an unqualified success. TRINITY NEWS 23.2.61

Several of RB's colleagues were made fun of behind their backs, some by even the most law-abiding. One Junior Dean was drenched from a carnival float; another found his car on the refectory steps. By contrast, I never heard RB derided, lampooned or vilified. It might be said that he was in himself funny enough, but I feel that there was also a respect for a fellow-child or escapee from the more formal aspects of fifties Trinity. 'Keep off the grass; wear your gown; get the girls out by four, then six, then nine; endure the inconsistencies of departmental marking policies and suffer the absurdities of the dreaded Little-Go.' Somehow, McDowell belonged to our Trinity, flourishing in spite of the notorious Board, its Regulations and reputations (summarized in the oral tradition of a lengthy song to the tune, 'Come to the Fair', to which members of the Hist, at least, were initiated in the small hours of an annual nocturnal gathering). JOSEPH GOY (1953)

ENCOUNTERS

There was an occasion when Alan Tait and I were talking late at night outside the doorway to Alan's staircase in Front Square, which was also McDowell's. Suddenly the Junior Dean erupted in a dressing-gown, demanding to know, 'Who is that?' There was a strict rule forbidding talking under people's windows late at night – 'It's a rule I always observe scrupulously myself and undergraduates would be severely reprimanded if they didn't. Good night!' Next day, when I approached him with a rather shamefaced apology, he waved it aside with a smile, and said confidentially, 'Now you know what I'm like when I'm roused!' DANIEL ROGERS (1954)
Professors Tait and Rogers were both lecturers.

In the 1950s, Dr McDowell seemed to be a fixture in Front Square, chatting to students as I passed by on my bike, to and from the Medical School. I knew that he was a Professor of History and I wish that I had chatted to him – there were so many people descended from famous, or infamous, families in the history of Ireland – or Great Britain – and I might have learned a lot. But at the time my mind was on other things. DR RUTH BLACKALL (1957)

I have memories of him fining undergraduates 7s 6d, for not wearing a gown! I also remember him with great affection, as one of the eccentrics of Trinity.
DOONIE SWALES (TOWNSEND) (1963)

In his role as JD, he was not to be taken for granted. My neighbour in Botany Bay, a very unsvelte Rob Ervine-Andrews, ignored a prohibition on his Morris Minor being parked in that enclave and was gated for a week. I remember my girlfriend and I smuggled him out through Front Gate one night, a difficult screening job. How he got back in again, I have no recollection.
ROGER KYNASTON (1966)

A student was sitting his exams in about 1960 and had forgotten his gown, so a friend tore the bottom half of his gown off and draped it over his shoulders. The invigilator saw the torn gown and threw him out of the exams, as he was not properly dressed. He went outside the exam hall and, to soothe his nerves, he lit his pipe, when around the corner came the Junior Dean with his hat on, who proceeded to summon the poor man ten shillings for smoking with a gown on!
ROBIN BURY (1963)

While I was in College I had rooms in No. 28 from 1960-64, the tenure on which I was able to extend from two to four years, by becoming a Chanter in College Chapel at the end of my second year. If RB had had his way, I would have been out, but through the support of the Senior Dean, J. La Touche Godfrey, who considered it a reasonable perk of the job (as a servant of the College), I resisted the

JD's demands and was able to keep my room until the end of the year after I graduated (having signed up for the LLB course).
RONALD FERGUSON (1972)

To us, in the early sixties, he seemed ancient, though he must have been considerably younger than we are now. He also symbolized a wise reliability, which served as a buffer between us and a harsher authority. Contrary to what might have been expected, since Dr McDowell, God bless him, had a reputation for strictness as well as fairness, it allowed us to indulge in outrageous behaviour. He twice bailed me out of the Garda pound where I'd been detained while the balance of my mind was fizzing with Guinness.
JOSE XUEREB (1963)

Sadly, I have few memories of him on either a personal or lecture level and I seemed to evade detection when committing crimes, so I did not cross him in his role as JD. He was always remarkable and I wish him many more happy years. DERMOT BEATTY (1957)

I suppose it was in the mid or late '50s that a new College rule forbade the riding of bicycles in Front Square. Alas, my Raleigh and I were spotted in cheekily rebellious trajectory and I was duly summoned to the Junior Dean's office. The memory of his admirably swift rebuke has stayed with me, 'If you don't keep the law, at least don't break it.' His shrewd parting shot was especially good, 'And don't try it on again!' I never did.
DR BRIAN ROBINSON (1959)

My memories of Dr McDowell hardly amount to tales or legends – just sayings, remarks or tiny episodes. One concerns my going to see him when I was first appointed, to say that the rooms that I had been allocated in Front Square were dark and dreary and that there was a much nicer set just vacant in the Rubrics. Rather than dismissing me as an arrogant young pup, he became quite defensive, as one who did not really notice these things, 'I wouldn't mind;' 'The College might

Front Square, *c.* 1950, by Bryan de Grineau

not like it;' 'But I wouldn't mind if I had a sort of paliasse in my office.' And so I got into the Rubrics.

DANIEL ROGERS (1954)

My memory dates from 1958–62, when I read Classics under Stanford, Wormel and Parks – a redoubtable trio of professors, which it would be hard to match. The Junior Dean was in evidence walking (if not gliding) around College, deep in conversation with himself. On becoming a Scholar, I moved into No. 7, Front Square and could then observe the JD on Commons, where I was paid to say Grace. I am not sure if the Junior Dean had time to eat other than on Commons or if he had the ability to prepare meals for himself. As a Classicist, I did not benefit from his lectures nor, as a moderate person, from his disciplinary powers.

FOSTER MURPHY (1962)

One evening, when I was at TCD in the mid to late sixties, I had returned to College, after a sip or two of the black stuff, only to discover that I had locked myself out of my rooms in New Square. No one else was in that evening – my 'wife' was elsewhere. When I enquired at Front Gate as to whether there was some way that I could be let in, the porters said that they could only assist me with the permission of the Junior Dean. They then handed me the 'phone and suggested that I contact the great man myself. Disappointed as I was that they did not appear to have the power to assist me directly, I had no alternative but to naively follow their advice. Now, although it was relatively early (at least for students), RB had either decided to retire early for the night or he was buried deep in some leather-bound tome of historical analysis. Anyway, it was after some time that he wearily answered. When I explained my predicament, he became quite agitated and enquired as to why I had bothered him at such an hour with what, to his mind, was a quite ridiculous request. When I told him in all innocence that I was only acting on the advice of the porters, he immediately retorted, 'Porters! Porters! For heaven's sake, you should never listen to the advice of servants!' RB thereupon asked to speak to the 'servants' and, after the latter were lambasted and humbled by his tongue for a bit, I was eventually assisted in getting back into my rooms.

GEOFF GOOLNIK (1969)

RULES AND REGULATIONS

DR McDOWELL COMMENTS:

My duties as a tutor and as Junior Dean did not weigh very heavily on a bachelor living in College, who was in a number of undergraduate circles. Indeed, for anyone interested in history, these duties taught me a number of useful lessons about administration and human nature. In practice, a consensus which combined a decent level of order with good humour prevailed, a state of affairs which might offend those who crave clear definitions and who are not altogether averse to what they are quick to see as issues of principle. It is a mistake to think that most of the work consisted of enforcing discipline 'policing.' In fact, it was largely a matter of granting permission and making amicable arrangements.

It should be said that it was an age when the undergraduates, generally speaking, took authority, paternal, school and academic, for granted. Junior members of the College accepted that the rules and regulations should be made and the place administered by their seniors – the dons. The undergraduates were by no means uncritical of
the way that the institution was run, but they were content for the time being to enjoy a welcome interlude between school and the hard work of the outside world. They might often have complained about aspects of existence, but the time for management was in the future. For the moment, they were content with the vigorous enjoyment of their intellectual, social and sporting lives. Also, the College régime was often tempered by a more or less adroit avoidance of the regulations by some of the more irritated. Moreover, there was an awareness on the part of the authorities that they were dealing with high-spirited young people – after all, junior and senior members of the College frequently exchanged opinions at meetings and parties. This demanded flexibility.

NIGHT ROLL

For male undergraduates (first year, I think) who lived in College, the process was to hold a roll-call at 10.00 each night and RB McD used to preside. GRAHAM WHEELER (1961)

I may be mixing up RB McDowell with his predecessor as Junior Dean, Dr Pyle. However, in the 1950s, when there was Night Roll, which was a requirement that students who lived in College should assemble in the entrance to the Dining Hall, to answer their names read out from the roll, to prevent them from leaving College for the remainder of the evening, Dr Pyle would, *if necessary*, turn a blind eye and when McDowell took over (in 1956), I believe that he carried on that humane tradition. COLIN TITE (1956)

It was one of the duties of the JD to turn up at Front Gate at 10 at night, to check the presence of a motley crew of undergraduates and to make sure that no one had gone AWOL during the previous 24 hours. Up turns the JD, wearing the Scarf and the Hat, with frost glinting on the cobbles of Front Square. It still amazes me to think that RB had to leave the warmth of his cosy rooms and his historical studies to carry out a roll-call at that hour of night, but so it was. JOHN GILL (1965)

RB's first roll-call was entertaining. 'Now, Gentlemen, we shall start with the letter "A".' With that, a large dog, wearing a Knights' tie, left the assembled company, walked up to the table, relieved himself against one of the legs and dutifully returned, to much applause. CHARLIE WEBB-PORTER (1957)

In September 1954, I moved into the top floor of No. 16, Botany Bay, to share rooms with Timothy Boyd-Maunsell (who, after graduating, ran the advertising section of *Readers Digest* for many years). For the first of the nightly roll-calls, we both turned up, wearing gowns and when Dr McDowell asked for 'Bs,' Timothy said, 'Boyd-Maunsell.'

The Campanile, *c.* 1950, by Bryan de Grineau

McDowell turned a jaundiced eye on him and remarked, 'Consider yourself an M.' DR HENRY SMITH (1957)

I really don't have any exciting anecdotes about the Junior Dean (as he will *always* be to me). My only brush with him was after having spent some fifteen months in rooms in College, without ever having attended Evening Roll Call, I was summoned, in late 1961, to explain myself. Having no excuse for what was an obligation on the part of resident students, I was punished, by having to attend each evening for three weeks. This I did and never went again!
DAVID LANGRIDGE (1963)

I am sure that you will have already had this story, but with a name like mine it is memorable! When doing the evening 10 o'clock roll-call, he called a Smyth, who did not reply. When the JD looked up and saw him, he asked why he did not reply and was told that it was because his name was Smythe and not Smyth. To which the JD replied, that the difference between Smyth and Smythe was the same as that between shit and shite! I'm afraid that this sounds better than it writes but I hope you will get the drift and will not take offence!
REV PETER BLACKWELL SMYTH (1963)

THE RIOT

DR McD RECALLS:

The Chief Steward had a photograph of me advancing against a cloud of smoke. The other day, something made me remember this photograph and wonder – how could I have been advancing against a cloud of smoke?

It was a late summer's evening in May 1968, with a palpable tension in the Dublin air. Trinity students had been revising over the last three to four months, in preparation for exams and – heaven forbid – Finals. A few students who had completed their exams came staggering back into college, drifting past Rotten Row and into Botany Bay in drunken song. At first one and then several College room windows opened, with a polite request to shut up, as some students were still sweating it out. When this request was met with strong verbal abuse, buckets of water showered over the drunken students.

Within seconds, a complete riot erupted in Botany Bay, as exam tension snapped and 300 pent-up students piled out of rooms into the Square. At this point a bright spark lit a smoke bomb, which engulfed the entire Square within minutes, whereupon an alert porter raised the Dublin Fire Brigade from Pearse Street, which came charging into College with all sirens blazing, 'Looking for the fire.' Within minutes, the entire College was in uproar and out of control.

Suddenly, out of the smoke appeared a familiar profile, of small stature with battered hat and a worn heavy coat. A single cry went up – 'JD' – and within two seconds the Square emptied and 300 students disappeared into thin air. It was as if a Genie had been gathered by an unseen hand and placed back in a bottle.

The JD didn't utter a word – then, or later. He did not need to. His simple presence defused the tension, the Dublin Fire Brigade disappeared as quickly as it had arrived and, miraculously, College returned to normal inside a few minutes. Never have I seen such student crowd control! What a presence!

MIKE SCHAAFSMA (1968)

These 'crowd control' skills, honed to perfection in Front Square, were to stand Dr McDowell in good stead in later years:

On a recent visit to us, he inspected a Bronze Age standing-stone in the fields and was beset suddenly by a herd of bullocks, which he faced down firmly and they backed off slowly!

PATRICK GUINNESS (1980)

EXAMINATION RULES

An eager young History student, who had been delving into the annals of TCD, arrived at the Examination Hall, to sit his first year exams. He strode in to find his allotted desk and then immediately requested the attention of the invigilator.

'Could you please tell me when the refreshments will be available?' he inquired.

The invigilator, a rather nervous junior lecturer, said that he would speak to someone about it. He returned five minutes later to inform the student that refreshments were not provided.

'But this is not right,' exclaimed the student excitedly, 'according to the Examination Rules of 1794, each student is entitled to a glass of porter during the sitting of examinations.' He then produced a copy of what appeared to be the 1794 rules, with the relevant sentence underlined and he refused to proceed with the exam until he got his porter. The JD was summoned. After a small commotion at the entrance to the Examination Hall between the JD and the junior lecturer, the JD was seen scuttling and chuntering to the library.

The JD returned to the Hall after fifteen minutes, with a pint of Guinness in one hand and an old brown volume in the other. He walked up to the desk of the student who had complained and set down the pint. The JD then opened the volume at a marked page and placed it on the student's desk. 'And according to these rules,' explained Dr McDowell, 'I am now fining you £5 for attending an examination without wearing your sword.'

ROBIN VERSO (1968)

WILD MEN

One dark winter's night in 1961, I had got back just in time to have the gate opened for me. Fortunately, I had seen my girlfriend to her digs that night. In those days, females had to be off the premises by 11 or had surreptitiously to spend the night in hiding. On this occasion, I had got into a solitary bed, when there came a tap at the window of my living-room. As it was several storeys up, at the top of the building in Front Square, it might have surprised me. But, remember, this was Trinity.

On the ledge outside, were two brawny undergraduates in dark sweaters. A closer look through the reflecting glass showed them to be bedecked with ropes. They looked very suspicious, so I opened the window and asked them in. It was no easy task for them to accept my invitation, since the sill, though broad, was cluttered with a cooking stove, kettle, frying pan, stew-pots and miscellaneous crockery and cutlery.

They told me that the Junior Dean, who had got wind of their exploits, had set the porters on them and asked if they could hide in my rooms. Instantly recognizing fellow spirits, I put my door on oaks and brewed up a pot of tea, nothing stronger being in stock at the time. I also put the lights out and we sat chatting in whispers in the dark for some time. Eventually, imagining the hue and cry to have been called off, I was about to switch the light back on and bid them goodnight when there was an authoritative knocking at the door. The chaps rushed into my bedroom and dived under the bed, making loud contact with the resident crockery.

I took my time shuffling to the door, which I opened a crack, trying to look as bleary-eyed as I could. The Junior Dean, who had frequently quaffed my claret in those rooms and was more a friend than an authority over me, here appeared in his Nazi guise. He told me that undergraduates, number unspecified, had been reported climbing the faces of the buildings and, despite my indignant protest, he insisted that the porters with him had a look in my rooms. I dreaded that the fugitives would choke on the fluff under the bed and sneeze, but nothing happened. I doubt if the porters were convinced of my angelic innocence, but, strangely, they went off on their hunt without bothering me any further.

I did not think anything of the incident at the time. I had forgotten it by the morning. I don't think that I ever knew the names of the two men, but I marvel at the brain's ability to recall detail so long stowed away with life's other trivial baggage. It was a contemporary of mine, Heather Lasky, who, at the Quartercentenary Dinner, cited the incident, which the two fellows must have recounted to her. In a flash I was back all those years, reliving it as if it had happened only a few minutes before. JOSE XUEREB (1961)

But who were the men and what was their story? Over to Heather Lasky, now living in Canada. Heather's comments lead quickly into darker and wilder realms:

POSSIBLE EXPLANATIONS

O N E : I have got a couple of possibly useful memories but I will also ask the husband (Jim O'Brien) to add his – I think that he may have been involved in the ropes story that Jose Xuereb referred to, except that there were no ropes. That one also involved Brian (GBR) Fisher, an attempted rooftop entry into a dance, with GBR Fisher hanging on to a down spout, which left the side of the building and crashed through a glass roof, the Gardai thinking that it was an attempt on the British Embassy and Jim, GBR and one other (at least) taking tea out of porcelain cups in Jose's flat. Why his flat I don't know. Unless he [Jose Xuereb] is talking of the time that Ronnie Wathen was thinking of using his climbing gear to escape, out of the window of his rooms, from Bob Barton who (naked) was axing down his door. I think, Jose may have the two incidents muddled. Anyway, I'll let Jim attempt the possible clarification. H E A T H E R   O '   B R I E N   (L A S K Y)   (1 9 6 1)

T W O : The incident with Ronnie Wathen (poet, wandering trouba-dour, uillean piper and mountaineer), the climbing rope and Bob Bar-ton, (both of whom I believe are now dead) was another stirring episode and RB was involved, as he removed Bob Barton from his rooms in Botany Bay because of it. Mind you, this was a pretty mild punishment for what Bob did, which was to reduce Ronnie's door to splinters with an axe, before marching back to his rooms, still stark naked, with the axe over his shoulder... D R   J I M   O ' B R I E N   (1 9 5 9)

T H R E E : (P O W E R   A N D   I N F L U E N C E   O F   T H E   B O A T   C L U B) It was not uncommon at closing time in those days in the Lincoln or O'Neill's of Suffolk Street or wherever, having heard of a party, wher-ever it might be, to make an attempt to gatecrash. That night we heard from someone about Jose Xuereb's party and, not having an invita-tion, three of us with nothing better to do, Brian Fisher (now a retired doctor in Yorkshire), Tom Molyneux (lives in Bray) and I decided to gatecrash. We attempted to do so by climbing up the back of the house to the third storey, where the party was being held. Unfortunately, en route, a drainpipe came away as Brian was halfway up and he, plus drainpipe fell onto a large skylight below, smashing some of the glass.

He sustained a concussion and a nasty cut to his hand, besides making a hell of a racket. We were at the back of the British Embassy and, unknown to us, at that time the terrorists had become quite active again. As a result of the noise and the proximity of the British Embassy, when the Gardaí were alerted, they surrounded the entire block. For some reason, a few of the Gardaí entered Jose's flat (with the party still going on) and, despite our best efforts to escape, picked us out from the window of the flat with a searchlight and ordered us to come up to the flat, providing ropes to help us do so.

Once the Gardai found out that we were not the IRA, but a few foolish half-cut TCD students, they treated it pretty much as a joke. Brian, of course, had to be taken to hospital to have his hand stitched and I am sure has the scars on that hand to this day. Tom and I were placed in a Garda car and taken off to, or maybe it was just towards, a Garda station somewhere for I don't think that we ever got there, as it turned out that one of the Gardaí came from Dunlavin, as did Tom Molyneux, and knew his family well. Anyway, we were all members of DUBC and the Gardaí had just started a rowing club and DUBC had given them considerable help with the start-up of their club. With this vital information, rather than arrest us, they drove us back to TCD, where we were all in residence.

I do remember at the party trying to placate them, by asking Jose to get them a cup of tea. This he did, in small delicate cups, with lemon instead of milk for their tea. I remember well one of the Gardaí, a large countryman ('culchie', in Dublin parlance), as so many of them were, looking at this small cup in his hand, turning to a colleague and saying, 'Jaysus, Mick, I never seen tay with a limon in it.'

I cannot remember 'RB', then the Junior Dean, being involved at all, but maybe he was. Certainly, there were no repercussions, but then he was always a great supporter of the Boat Club, God knows why, and came to most of our often pretty wild social occasions, which he always seemed to enjoy. DR JIM O'BRIEN (1961)

ESCAPADES

Towards the end of the fifties, Andrew Bonar-Law orchestrated a series of daring pranks, which, although they did not directly *involve the Junior Dean, are definitely not forgotten. Among the most celebrated of these were:* 'The Film Crew Trolley', 'The Smoke Bomb in the Campanile', 'The Examination Hall Organ' *and* 'The Reading Room Wall'.

Here, Keith Ferguson describes The Film Crew Trolley event:

You, I hope, have some of the Andrew Bonar-Law antics. The late 1950s were great days, just before the change began in earnest, in the early 1960s. I saw a little, as I finished my PhD in 1964. The Film Crew – I am hopeless on names of films, but it was one of those classics that were being partially shot in College. Not *Educating Rita*, it was much later. Anyway, as I recall, they had a trolley like a large car-chassis on bit wheels of motor car size, on which they mounted the camera and the cameraman sat on and the camera could move in and out, etc., mounted on this. It was the late 1950s, not the 1990s!

Come the Whit Bank Holiday, I think, the film crew parked their trolley in the Parade Ground and disappeared. As I understand it, our good friend AB-L organized a group of worthies and they towed it up College Park into the Fellows Garden (AB-L seemed to have keys to most doors and gates, one was led to believe), around to the back of the Exam Hall. A rope was lowered from the roof and attached to the trolley (car-chassis size) and it was pulled up the Fellows Garden end of the Exam Hall. It got caught on the parapet, I believe, and the noise attracted somebody, either in the Provost's House or Garden (it was early June and people were out and about after dark). The porters appeared and searched and found nothing, the trolley being lashed to the chimney at this point and the culprits having departed back through the roof of the run of rooms, between the Exam Hall and Front of College, from where they could drop onto the fourth floor. In fact, I believe that there was a set of rooms which had a 'loft door,' but I may have imagined this. Where the rope came from I can't recall, but it was NOT AB-L's, that is for sure!

The trolley hung below the parapet, wheels on wall astride windows and roped to the chimney for certainly one whole day if not two, in full view of Grafton Street. That is, if you were in Grafton

Street and looking for a trolley hanging from the Exam Hall roof! I believe that AB-L thought that it had been spotted and was left there as a trap. It appeared not and when he was satisfied that it was in fact feasible to get it on to the roof of the Exam Hall, he recruited more worthies, including my 'wife' at the time. They gained access to the Exam Hall roof again, through the loft of, possibly, No. 23. The trolley was eased over the parapet with great difficulty and was placed on the roof of the Exam Hall. College was not at all amused and thought this a prank too far, as it cost a bomb to have it removed from the Exam Hall roof without further damage to the roof and the damage done to it already was seriously expensive. To my knowledge, they never caught anybody, but they probably knew the culprit or the brains behind the prank and they made it known that they were not amused. Long-winded and probably horribly inaccurate, but that is how I remember it. I can still see my 'wife' laughing and laughing, drunk with exhilaration. Four pints in O'Neill's, I can attest, did not have as stimulating an effect on him!

DR IK FERGUSON OBE (1964)

Andrew Bonar-Law comments:

From memory, I suppose that Keith Ferguson's tale is more or less correct. Although I can't see exactly where RB McD comes into the frame. I believe that the trolley was left belayed to the chimney, perpendicular to the ground, just below the parapet, not because the miscreants were disturbed, but simply because they were unable to lever it over the slight overhang. He is right when he says that it was visible from the bottom of Grafton Street, but only really if one knew where and for what to look. The following night, armed with a couple of short scaffolding poles, the cart was levered over and wheeled to the front of the roof, to be visible from Front Square. Great care was taken not to damage any slates. The car, being rubber-tyred, was wheeled easily to its final resting-place, with no damage to the roof. I did hear that the clerk-of-work's men did break slates, when removing the offending article. They were always a clumsy lot. The rope, I believe, was supplied by Ronnie Wathen and was one of his discarded climbing ropes. Ronnie, now unfortunately dead, was the only non-Scholar on the job. He was a sizar. Of the Scholars in residence, the only one who refused the call to duty was David Spearman, known thereafter as 'Honest Dave'. His 'wife', W.B. Clarke, was unable to coax him out. THE HON ANDREW BONAR-LAW (1959)

THE ORGAN IN THE EXAMINATION HALL
Another one, perhaps not directly related to McDowell, but of the same vintage, was when the guests for a graduation were greeted with soothing organ music as they entered the Examination Hall. The students, the lecturers and the other VIPs also filed in and took their places. It took some time to register that no one was playing the organ and they couldn't locate the source of the sound. After a great deal of running about, someone found a loudspeaker and pulled the wires out of it. JOHN WILSON (1971)

I recall RB's reaction to the organ playing at Commencements, as he rushed to the organ loft to see if there was someone inside. When the dust had cleared, Basil Chubb made a very magnanimous gesture, in returning the record used – Bach's 'Pasacalia & Fugue' – giving thanks at the same time that 'Jailhouse Rock' hadn't been the chosen record. AB-L

DR McDOWELL COMMENTS:
At a Commencements, when the organ was out of commission for repairs, suddenly, when the procession was starting off from the platform, music began to emanate from the organ. This was very surprising! It turned out that Bonar-Law had put a record player in the organ, but it was very confusing at the time to work out what was happening. The music, I should add, was very suitable to the occasion!

More from AB-L:

THE 'NO PARKING' SIGN
Do you remember a copy of *TCD* that illustrated RB's perambulations around the Front Square? I have a copy somewhere. I thought

that they were very accurate, for I am minded of one night around two or three in the morning, when a self-standing 'No Parking' sign about four foot tall on a relatively heavy base was being hoisted into position, to stand on the inside of the pediment above the entrance to the Exam Hall. The sign was in position and the placers were about to climb away, when RB came out of his rooms and proceeded to potter around the Square weaving, often retracing his steps, tossing his keys and muttering the while. The climbers simply sat, with their legs hanging over the ledge, hoping that he wouldn't look up, until, still muttering, he retired once again. The *TCD* artist had got it to a T. (See page 58)

THE BRICK DOOR

An episode, that apparently did not come to the notice of the JD, was quite unusual. I arrived at the Reading Room one morning, to join a group that were unable to get into the building. The reason became apparent as I got to the steps. The door had been bricked up very artistically, leaving us absolutely nonplussed. There was nothing I could do, except totter on my narrow heels back across the cobbles and recover from the shock with coffee at Switzers. By mid-morning, the bricks had been removed and the Reading Room was back in business. It seems that a pile of bricks near the Reading Room had attracted the attention of Andrew Bonar-Law and Jammy Clinch, who had been unable to resist the temptation to make use of them.
BEULAH GARCIN (WELLS) (1958)

FIREWORKS

I have recollections of RB and the College Porters hunting down fire crackers that had been placed strategically around College and fused to go off every twenty minutes or so, for a number of hours.
COLIN SMYTHE (1963)

In the winter of 1958 to 59 there was a fireworks craze in College. This resulted in a very unpleasant accident in Front Square, where family and friends were gathered for Commencements. An aspiring engineer and a chemically-inclined natural scientist were rusticated for

the Hilary Term by Junior Dean McDowell for perpetrating this and a number of other incidents. His comment on the matter, said to have been made at High Table on Commons, was, 'Getting drunk or going to bed with a woman is one thing, but fireworks are just childish.'
DR I.K. FERGUSON OBE (1964)

THE LORRIES

There was a tale of a jolly student jape, featuring a convoy of lorries or vans ordered up in the JD's name, for relocating the Library stock. I can remember nothing more. DAVID GILLIAT (1961)

THE ENGINEERS

In about 1946, there was a loud explosion in the lecture theatre on the ground floor of the Engineering School, where a lecture by Dr McDowell for Divinity students was in progress. A few moments later, he was seen leaving the building at speed. In an adjacent lecture room, some 30 Engineering students were being lectured by that redoubtable disciplinarian, Professor Purser, who (a) did not like his lecture being interrupted, (b) did not like the thought of any damage being done to his Engineering School and (c) was known to have some earthy views about Divinity students as a group. So, when he put down his piece of chalk with ominous firmness on the lectern and walked out of the room with measured tread, to investigate the noise and possible damage, the Engineering class feared that whatever might happen to others, the rest of their lecture would be a decidedly tense affair.

Imagine their surprise when Professor Purser returned, smiling. 'Ah,' he said, 'there has been an explosion, Dr McDowell has disappeared and there is a slight smell of brimstone.' At which witticism, the Engineering students, much relieved, obliged with generous laughter. JOHN JOHNSTON (1946)

10/10/02: email to John Johnston, 'Who did it?'
10/10/02: email to Editor, 'Who else could it be, but those sinful Divinity students!'

DR McDOWELL COMMENTS:

I must begin by declaring a bias: for very many years I have considered practical joking a waste of time, which may hurt people's feelings or damage property. Putting a car on the roof of the Examination Hall was, I admit, spectacular. But was it worth it? Putting a tape
into the organ was brilliant. It was exhilarating and hurt nobody. I
am fairly certain that 'authority' in College did not see these practical
jokes as part of a destabilising campaign. Rather, they are incidents of
the sort that are bound to happen, from time to time, especially as the
forces of law and order were, at night, weak, compared to the size in
area and the population of College. But then the Bursar was quite
rightly pressing me about the cost of policing.

ANIMALS IN COLLEGE

SNAKES, A MONKEY, SOME DOGS AND A MOUSE

Animals were not allowed within the precincts of College without
the prior approval of the Junior Dean. During his speech to the
London Dining Club, in February 2003 (see page 139), Dr McDowell recalled requests that he had received to accommodate non-
humans – a pair of snakes (non-venomous) had once required, for
reasons of botanical interest, temporary residence in Botany Bay. As
an incentive to obtaining his consent, the reptiles' owner had offered
Dr McDowell permission to wind the snakes around his arms and
head whenever he liked. In the event, the reptiles stayed in the Bay for
over two months, causing no problems whatsoever.

However, one other incident of this nature was somewhat less
effectual. Returning to College one evening, Dr McDowell noticed a
visitor, short of stature and walking with a peculiar gait, being accompanied by two undergraduates. Closer investigation revealed that this
was in fact a monkey. Its owners wished it to stay the night. Now it
so happened that Dr McDowell had a soft spot for monkeys, having
had an uncle who kept one as a pet. For hereditary reasons, possibly,
permission was given for the simian to stay overnight, providing that
it left the premises first thing in the morning. All went well while the
JD was present, the animal remaining calm and displaying com-

mendable deference in the presence of authority. However, as soon as the Junior Dean had left the room, all changed. The monkey went wild, smashing plates and everything else, so that its owners quickly regretted having made such extravagant arrangements for its comfort. They were only too pleased to depart at dawn, taking their guest to more permanent digs in Dublin Zoo. A . L .

How well I remember, while in residence at Trinity College in the mid 1960s, temporarily harbouring a stray dog in rooms at 36.01 New Square, contrary to College regulations, which forbade the keeping of animals in residences. In due course, this 'misdemeanour' came to the attention of the Junior Dean, Dr RB McDowell, who promptly sent around a notice demanding the princely sum of £2, by way of a fine for flouting College rules.

A few days later, my roommate, John Nickson, sent out invitations for a wine and cheese party – remember those many wonderful parties – to celebrate his appointment as editor of *Trinity News*, if my memory serves me right. It was customary to invite the JD to such social events – indeed, permission had to be sought from him to hold such an event in your rooms – and he duly turned up. I gather that he always showed up at such events, finding it impossible to resist a captive audience, well-lubricated and eager to collogue.

Being rather partial to the 'water of life' whisky, the JD was plied with a generous few drams and he quickly engaged in conversation with John and myself, as we leaned against the mantelshelf. The subject of pets in rooms came up – 'Totally against College regulations and just as heinous as harbouring a woman in rooms after 10.00 p.m.,' he stated, quite firmly and seriously, I think.

However, having determined that our four-legged waif and stray had been duly despatched to a good home, his countenance changed and he beamed through his grimy spectacles, as only the JD could, picked up the notice for the, as yet, unpaid fine, which had been left on display upon the mantelshelf and stuffed it into his coat pocket with one hand, while proffering his empty glass with the other. As the glass was liberally replenished, he beamed again, as only the JD could, muttered something about 'quid pro quo' and meandered off

– both physically and verbally – on a different tangent, as he engaged another group of partygoers. DR REGINALD PARTON (1968)

I found a small stray dog in Trinity; it had been hanging around New Square all day, looking very hungry and eyeing me piteously each time I passed by, so I picked it up and took it into somebody's rooms and asked a passing Veterinary student to have a look at it. He said that it was just very hungry and exhausted, so I fed it, took it back to my flat and washed it. Next morning, and from then on, I took it in a basket to lectures, artfully covered with a cloth. One lecturer did notice it and asked, tartly, what was its name and where was its gown.

My nemesis overtook me however; I was walking across Front Square, carrying my covered basket and flanked by four stalwarts from the Rugby Club, when the Junior Dean's distinctive figure came over to me. My four brave escorts melted into the surrounding buildings, leaving me to face the JD alone. His observant eye had obviously noticed my little dog some time previously and this was his first opportunity to speak to me. 'Miss Wells,' he said, 'if you do not get rid of that dog, I shall forbid you the precincts of the University.' There wasn't much choice, so my little dog went to live with my parents and enjoyed a long and happy life with them.

Some time later, I was walking towards Front Gate and saw ahead of me a friend, carrying a rather heavy suitcase. When I caught up with him, just outside Front Gate, he stopped, put down the suitcase and opened the lid. To my amazement, out jumped a dog. Nick's explanation was that he had won the animal in a raffle, but couldn't have it in his rooms. I wonder if the Junior Dean had had some hand in expelling it, too? BEULAH GARCIN (WELLS) (1958)

I had rooms in College from 1954 to 1958, in No. 2 for the first two years and in Botany Bay for the second two. Dr McDowell was Junior Dean. Freshmen were required at that time to attend a roll-call at the front of the Dining Hall every evening, to attend Chapel on Sundays and to be back in College by (I think) 11 p.m. every night. Any misdemeanour brought forth a note from the Junior Dean which began,

'The Junior Dean presents his compliments...' and required one to explain oneself and, perhaps, to pay a fine. One of my colleagues was required to call on Dr McDowell in these circumstances, in his sparsely furnished rooms in Front Square. He found Dr McDowell and a mouse having breakfast together. Dr McDowell was attacking a loaf at one end of the table, while the mouse was consuming a large chunk of bread at the other. BILL HIPWELL (1959)

WOMEN IN COLLEGE

It was still a man's world in the Golden Era; as late as the 1950s, women were not allowed in rooms, even in daylight! Eventually, things thawed a bit and ladies could visit until 6 p.m., then 9 p.m., then 11.30. Since 1972, they can live in! But in the Golden Era, the penalties for that most nefarious crime – staying overnight – were severe and I remember a girl in my year and her companion actually being sent down. Others, it was rumoured, got away with it, so they may have been luckier, or more practised – or tipped the skip enough – not to get caught. A.L.

It is hard to believe now, that, like the monastic settlement on Mt Athos, where no female animal is allowed to set foot, the male citadel of Trinity was kept pure from 6 o'clock in the evening, when the last woman was ushered through Front Gate. TRINITY NEWS (1980)

I was one of the Junior Dean's confidants. But, one day, to my surprise and chagrin, he arrived at No. 18 Botany Bay in the afternoon, to carry out an official inspection. My girlfriend and wife of forty-three years, Gilda Hensley, was making lunch for my roommate, John Campbell and me, and had to make a hasty retreat under my bed. McDowell, being McDowell, lingered on, talking to John and me about the world in general, leaving Gilda crouched under the bed for a very long time indeed! I often wonder what might have been McDowell's reply ... if she had emerged from under the bed!
LORD HASKINS (CHRIS HASKINS) (1959)

I suspect that many students' memories of him may well be of times when they thought they'd got the better of him. Memorable to the individual, but much less so to those to whom it is told. In 1963 women had recently been allowed to stay until 11.30 p.m. in College, as guests of those male students living there, but they definitely had to be out by that deadline. Front Gate was officially closed at 11.30 p.m. and names were taken after that. On this occasion, I was walking a friend with her bicycle to Front Gate when, just as we were passing No. 30, the clock struck 11.30 p.m. and we had the misfortune of also passing the JD at that exact moment. Damn. What to do? We quickened our pace and at Front Gate my friend got on her bike and cycled into the night, while I walked back across Front Square, to be greeted by the Junior Dean, who obviously was waiting for me.

'What do you mean by it, Smythe?'

'What do I mean by what, sir?'

'You were with that lady. I was there beside you when the clock struck and you did absolutely nothing about it.'

With his use of that term to describe my guest, I thought that I had a way out. It was worth a try. 'Sir, I was very well aware of that, but I thought that it would be ungentlemanly to tell her to get on her bicycle and peddle like mad.' I was sufficiently pleased with that answer that I did not take too much notice of his reply, except to be aware that it had worked. I'd avoided any disciplinary action and, more importantly, further verbal castigation from him (at which form of punishment I have never met anyone more accomplished), beyond an admonition to be more careful about the time in future. He doubtless forgot the incident almost immediately, but the memory of that meeting is almost as clear to me now, as when it occurred, as is the sense of what I thought of as the winning of a skirmish.

COLIN SMYTHE (1963)

I was allowed, in 1962, to entertain a woman in my rooms until 11.00 p.m. and we then had to get across to the last bus in the following twenty-seven minutes! We've been happily married for thirty-seven years!

FOSTER MURPHY (1962)

DR McDOWELL COMMENTS:

Just after I was appointed Junior Dean, a very sagacious Senior Fellow told me that one of the most important attributes of a Junior Dean was not to see things!

A PARTY IN ROOMS

My own case history is of, I think, a unique invitation to Dr McDowell to my rooms in Botany Bay, to keep a party going well past the curfew, with actual wine and real women. This 'real' party was in 18.01 on the ground floor of the Bay, when I was in rooms from 1964 to 1966-ish, shared, first with an engineer called Eddie and my second 'wife' (Dr) Michael Moore, whom I never heard of again. I think that the party, 7 p.m. to 9 p.m., or however long I could get the JD to drag it out, was co-hosted by another medical student.

Our mission was to have our idea of a proper party, which would be in the evening, after Commons, would have wine, not beer, which was primarily to entertain ladies and in our snug rooms was to last much longer than the dreaded early women-out time. In a brilliant piece of original thought, I invited Dr McDowell and, to our astonished delight, he accepted. So I laid on a Senior Sophister in History and instructed the ladies, in a rota, to look after the JD, which was of huge entertainment to our most honoured guest. Well, there is more detail, but the gist is that Dr McDowell enjoyed the company of the lady students so much that he stayed on and on, exactly to plan. Meanwhile, outside the open windows, a porter and then two porters and then the Head Porter prowled maliciously up and down the Bay, completely stymied in their task to throw out the women and reprimand us. I watched them peer through the window nearest the door and home in on the JD. Curses! From the porters' point of view, 'For God's sake, the darn JD was actually in Mr Youell's rooms with "wimmin",' he was gesticulating in full flow and he was not leaving any time soon, getting on for two hours after the 9 p.m. curfew.

There was no man in the whole of Dublin who would interrupt RB McDowell and certainly the Head Porter was not a man to so discourteously knock on our black door, to remind the JD of the hour. In fact, maybe an error here, it is possible that the Head Porter did bring 'the party to set a standard for all parties' to an end, with a black scowl to me and by whispering in the great man's ear. In fact, we passed locking-door time at Trinity Hall and we escorted appropriate ladies by taxi, with the JD's apologies – which, for once, was true. The she-wolf of The Liz, Melissa Stanford, was, astonishingly, my girlfriend at the time and she led the cabal back.

You will agree that it is a story definitely from the, hitherto unknown, archives. I could write some more on the huge smiles for the ladies and on the fervid, breathless, wildly gesticulating JD, ranging over every topic known only to Dr RB McDowell.
DR ADRIAN YOUELL (1968)

1952. Trinity Week party in No. 16, Botany Bay, first floor room, occupied by Desmond Mully and Bill Doughty. We served a very popular punch – some might have called it a 'Mickey Finn'! Professor McDowell had broken his leg, or certainly injured it in some way, but it was on the mend. He had equipped himself with a stout walking stick. The rooms had a large pair of antlers, inherited by us and, of course, donated to the next inhabitants, in due course. One of our guests found the walking stick and hooked it onto the antlers and, when the time came for RB to leave, the stick could not be found. By this time, most of the guests had had several glasses of punch and the search faculty no doubt was severely impaired. Professor McDowell was eventually restored to his walking stick and, having chatted to all of his favourite sportsmen and to many of the most attractive female undergraduates in College, he descended to the ground level of Botany Bay and, as we learned later, regained his rooms in Front Square quite safely. SIR WILLIAM DOUGHTY (1953)

In my final years at TCD (1970–72), the Junior Dean wasn't the Junior Dean (!) – it was a chap from the Botany Department, but nonetheless McDowell continued as the Junior Dean, as indeed he has even in retirement. It must have been hell for his successors, that they could never make the position their own. I am sure that the more recent generation of students are unaware of his contribution to the traditions of TCD. STEPHEN RICHARDSON (1972)

ATTEMPTS TO OUTWIT THE JD (FOILED)

*I*n even such a law-abiding age, there was no shortage of intrepid
spirits anxious to test the status quo, breaking, bending and twisting the regulations, to see just how far they could go and, above all,
trying to outwit the Junior Dean. With the appointment of Dr Mc-
Dowell as JD, most of them found thet had met their match. A . L .

DR MCDOWELL RECALLS:
THE FLOWERS

I remember this quite clearly. Shortly after I became Junior Dean,
the porter from Front Gate rang, to say that a bunch of flowers had
arrived for me. Fortunately, I remembered the Berners' Street hoax of
about 1820, when a well-known wag (Hook?) arranged for a great
variety of items – a fire engine and a hearse – to arrive at about the
same time at a house occupied by an elderly gentleman in that street.
I instructed the Chief Steward to inform all the gates of College that
anyone bringing any deliveries for me should be directed back to
base. This meant that nothing reached my rooms! It was a very obvious idea. The Chief Steward, who was very quick off the mark, saw
that this was carried out and nothing got delivered all day!

THE INVITATIONS

I received a telephone call from an irate lady who was the widow of
a colonel. Word had reached her that hundreds of undergraduates had
been sent invitations to her house, in a remote area outside Dublin.
Needless to say, she wanted this stopped! I put it about on the Trinity grapevine – a very efficient form of communication – that nobody
was to go there and only one person turned up. Luckily, the news had
got around and I had not been at all sarcastic with her, for she was
my hostess at a party, given by her brother, the following week.

THE GARDAÍ

On another day, I was telephoned by a man with an extra strong Irish
accent, who told me that he was the Garda Sergeant for Stepaside,

Front Gate, *c.* 1950, by Bryan de Grineau

somewhere in the foothills near Dublin. He said that 300 undergraduates had been arrested, for being drunk and disorderly. I expressed great solicitude and asked if he could give me the telephone number of his station. At once the Irish accent dropped and I heard the caller in an agitated voice saying, 'He wants to know the number of the station!' and I put down the telephone!

THE PORTERS

The college porters, attired in formal uniforms, monitored everyone and everything entering and leaving the university, especially going past the Porters' Lodge at 'Front Gate,' where they were based. They were directly responsible to the Junior Dean for security within College, acting, to some extent, as 'Bobbies on the beat'.

A story of McDowell's own is worth recording. When the French were retreating at Waterloo, the Colonel of the battalion that had defended the farmhouse where there had been so much fighting, remembered to congratulate one of his men. The man was very tall and strong, with long arms; he had several times led a party that repulsed the French at the gate of the farmyard; several times he had closed the gate, or blocked it with débris; he had lifted Frenchmen and thrown them out. To the Colonel's, 'Well done, my man,' he replied, 'Sure it was nothing, your honour. I was the porter for five years at the Front Gate of Trinity College!'

DR W.E. VAUGHAN, Dept of Modern History, TCD (1967)

The Junior Dean, Dr RB McDowell, and Professor Basil Chubb, 1966, 'On the steps of the Dining Hall'.

PHOTO: CHRIS JOHNSTON

Sartorial Consistency

A STYLE OF HIS OWN

Of all of the stories that people tell about RB, the most prevalent concern his style of dress. Perfectly conventional attire for a gentleman, he wore his ensemble of hat, coat, suit and scarf (and the keys) with a consistency that made him instantly recognisable, anywhere, for he wore them regardless of climate, temperature or place. One tale, that went the rounds for years, concerned a visit to Greece by Professor Stanford and a group of students. Lightly embellished, the story goes, that the group, in Athens, at the height of summer, pause, temporarily defeated by the sizzling heat, to melt and/or expire in some shade. One, more alert than his companions, shouts, 'Look!' (in Greek!) forcing his fellows to focus sufficiently to follow his pointing finger, to where, on the horizon, has appeared a small dark figure, proceeding with an unmistakable rhythm, well wrapped up in a hat, coat and scarf. Fearful that they may be in the presence of a mirage, the group gaze mesmerized, as the figure approaches, moving ever faster, oblivious of the heat, deep in conversation with himself, before passing at speed with a notional, but courteous, acknowledgment of their presence. A.L.

I remember meeting RB coming down Grafton Street, on what was probably the hottest day of summer. I suspect that I was on my way to Davy Byrnes. I was, frankly, dying of the heat, but RB was clad in a sensible flannel shirt, a pullover, a waistcoat, a tweed sports coat, a scarf and overcoat and he remarked, in passing, 'It gets very cold in the evenings!' DR CHRISTOPHER PETIT (1956)

I understand that, on being questioned about the ever-present over-coat, hat (of which I am always reminded, when I see Gene Hackman in *The French Connection* – an unlikely coupling!) and scarf, he revealed that, having been presented naked to the world at birth, he had vowed, there and then, never to be under-dressed again! PETER BOWLES (1966)

I was at College from 1938 to 44 and I remember RB as an old-fash-ioned eccentric, dressed in a long rainproof cloth coat, always with trilby hat and umbrella and talking to friends in the Front Square. As a narrow-minded medical student, I thought that he was a dotty aca-demic! R. DESMOND LEWIS (1944)

I will always remember him walking briskly around Front Square in mid-summer, with his hat pulled down and his scarf pulled up around his neck! DERMOT BEATTY (1957)

RB has the amazing quality of never worrying what he looks like – or maybe he just takes great pains to always look the same. He hasn't really changed in the fifty odd years that I've known him and I saw him ten days ago. HENRY CLARK (1950)

He was certainly a well-known character, who was always around. I was fascinated by his appearance since he wore a darkish suit, a volu-minous woollen scarf, wound several times around his neck, and a distinctive green trilby hat. He walked in rapid steps (a bit like a bird) and often scanned the Front Square scene by periodically turning through 360 degrees as he sped along. He seemed to be a keen con-versationalist and he had a high-pitched, earnest, rapid-fire style of delivery. ULRIC SPENCER (1951)

After I graduated, I visited Dublin frequently. If I didn't have a 'sighting' of the Junior Dean, still in the same hat, scarf and coat, I was disappointed. It was rumoured that he slept in the hat and the scarf.
DOONIE SWALES (TOWNSEND) (1963)

He had a slightly less shabby coat, which he called his Belfast coat! There was, too, an almost smart coat, for trips to London.
HENRY CLARK (1950)

In a 1969 *Harpers & Queen* issue devoted to Ireland, he was famously described as resembling 'an Arab in a dust storm,' due to his many layers of clothing. His hat and scarf were removed, with reluctance, on the warmest days. Invariably, a waistcoat and/or jumper was worn underneath his suit. He was reputed, no doubt scurrilously, to wear three pairs of socks. Much later, we found out that he had suffered a terrible illness in 1918 and that his layers were a sensible precaution. Now that too many antibiotics are known to be a bad thing, his dress may come back into vogue, as a form of preventative medicine.
PATRICK GUINNESS (1980)

In my last two years at Trinity, I lived on the same staircase as Dr McDowell and inevitably saw a good deal of the strange figure in a drab suit, sporting four inches of pyjama bottom below the trouser cuff, on his head a pork-pie hat that a charity shop would disdain. He used to skitter purposefully along, as if his brakes were on the blink, jingling a bunch of keys and muttering obliviously to himself, his upper jaw doing all the work. JOSE XUEREB (1963)

I remember him going round College muttering to himself, always wearing a huge 'Dr Who' scarf (whatever the weather!).
SHEILA AYLING (1955)

He not only invariably wore odd socks, but he had a habit of unbuttoning his suit while lecturing and then his shirt, on at least one occasion to reveal pyjamas underneath. Despite this, he managed to date some of the prettiest girls in College.
DR JILL SHEPPARD (ROBBINS) (1957)

The Chapel and the Dining-Room, *c.* 1950, by Bryan de Grineau

My main memory is of a rather untidy figure, who normally seemed to wear three waistcoats, summer and winter! BOB STAMP (1955)

The JD often went to student parties, in his ragged coat and battered trilby hat. One host asked him if he would like to hang up his hat and coat. 'No, thank you, I'd rather not, in case someone else takes them away,' said the JD. Every now and again, though, his aunt from Belfast would come to Dublin and get him a new outfit.
CANON PETER NORTON (1961)

Scene: The Common Room, early 1950s:
Enter RBMcD looking rather 'cooth'.
ME: 'You're looking very smart today!'
RBMcD: 'Yes, I'm going to see my tailor and I don't like to hurt his feelings!' GRAHAM MCCARTHY (1952)

I can remember his attendances in the College Chapel, where he would be present attired in the usual decrepit overcoat, on top of which he would wear a decaying surplice, with threads hanging from it. On top of this collage, he would wear a decaying scarf. I remember an occasion attending divine service, accompanied by my visiting former headmaster, a rather respectable and severe Scotsman. I remember finding it impossible to keep a straight face, when Dr McDowell appeared in full fig, to read the lesson. Instead of walking in a straight line towards the lectern, Dr McDowell would wander from one side of the aisle to the other, until he reached the appropriate point where, needless to say, he read superbly.
GAVIN LLOYD (1964)

I remember, too, his remarking that he thought that one should always wear a suit in a capital city. No mention of whether or not one should sleep in it. DANIEL ROGERS (1954)

Neither being an historian nor ever having fallen foul of the Junior Dean, my only real memories of him are of the pork-pie hat and scarf steaming through the College. It is, however, impossible to think of him other than as 'The Junior Dean'. It was as if he wore his office like a mantle. Indeed, the sartorial combination of hat, scarf and office were as iconic as Sherlock Holmes's deerstalker, pipe and Ulster. DAVID R. WATSON (1969)

He loved his gown, which was in two parts and which had belonged to his father. SIR WILLIAM DOUGHTY (1953)

He was among the most visible staff members, standing in Front Square, noisily advising or debating with two or three students, or, more commonly, rushing (gliding, darting, scuttling, hurtling) between his rooms and the Reading Room, where he feverishly worked, or organized elaborate book withdrawals. Day and night, in all seasons, he ran, rather than walked, in the same long overcoat, scarf, NHS-type glasses and battered pork-pie hat, balancing an incredible column of books before him, yet somehow managing to see past them, avoiding obstacles by a hair's breadth. JOSEPH GOY (1953)

I am glad that the JD is still with us. I had little to do with him but retain a vivid memory of a man in black, including overcoat, in all weathers, his hat and horn-rims ... frenziedly chuntering to himself, with bunch-of-keys accompaniment. DAVID GILLIAT (1961)

We went to a lunch in Oxford fifteen to twenty years ago, with my friend, Louisa, and her father, George Quin, Bishop of Down and Dromore. He had been a contemporary of RB as a student and greeted him, saying, 'I see you haven't found your comb yet!' MOIRA GILL (WILLIAMSON) (1965)

I've just remembered: I stole his hat on the way out of one of his lectures when I was a student and gave it to Terry Brady, who needed it to do his McDowell take-off for a Players Revue (Tony Colgate used to do an even better one). I wondered what kind of new headgear he would come up with. I think that he bought a replacement, but it immediately looked like the old one. How did he do it? HEATHER O'BRIEN (LASKY) (1961)

Nooo! Even Tony Colgate said that my take-off was better than his! I had McDowell's hat for years after I left. It was no easy task – pinching a royal crown would be child's play, compared with coming by a Dr McDowell original. Word had it that his hat never left his head – not even when the great man was a-bed – which, of course, could go some way to explaining its particularly distinctive shape. So, my first attempts at hat-napping failed miserably.

The nearest that I came to success was at a party attended by the great man, when, at the end, I found his hat on a chair. Before I could nick it, a whirlwind arrived somewhat breathlessly beside me, in search of its head-gear. 'Ah, Mr er – Mr er – Mr *Brady*,' the whirling dervish said. 'I see you appear I see to have er to have er to have *found* er my *hat*.' 'Yes indeed, Dr McDowell,' I replied. 'But I'm sorry to say you seem to have sat on it.' 'Oh my oh yes oh my-my,' he said, regarding his even more dented and damaged chapeau. 'Indeed I have. Indeed I have I appear – to have sat upon it. Ah well,' he sighed, putting it back on his head, 'Ah well it was just as well I wasn't wearing it at the time.' TERENCE BRADY (1961)

The Professor likes to keep well wrapped up at all times. A three-piece suit, a cardigan and a long grey woollen muffler are his normal attire. On arriving at the Reform Club in July, a distinctly pompous majordomo assured me that he had yet to arrive and ushered me into a waiting-room. I then went to the cloakroom. A battered brown trilby hat and yards and yards of muffler trailing half way across the cloakroom assured me that the Professor was in fact in the club. A moment later, he greeted me. ROBERT BAILEY-KING (19XX)

Dr. McDowell's Path to the Reading Room

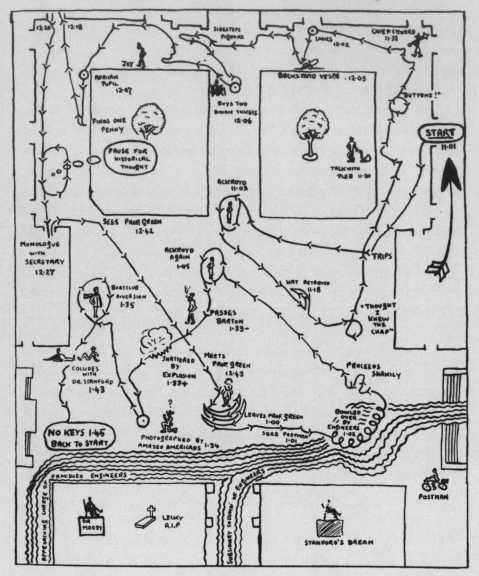

'Doctor McDowell's Path to the Reading Room', courtesy of The Publications Committee. This map appeared in *TCD – A College Miscellany,* in November 1956.

Great Trinity Eccentric

Although it is over sixty years since I last saw RB, he is still very vivid in my mind's eye and ear. When I think of him, two other men of genius immediately come to mind: Alan Turing and Glen Gould. I suppose that it is because of the ever-present coat and scarf. During my time in College, I was a member of the Phil. Had I belonged to the Hist, which tended to suit the historians and politicians, I might have known him better. GEORGE PARKER (1940)

You have of course heard the one, which everybody knows, of how McD was heard to observe how curious it was that there were no academic eccentrics nowadays. MAURICE CRAIG (1944)

It is Dr McDowell the man – or, perhaps more properly, Mr McDowell the character – that I would praise. Not that Dr McDowell the lecturer, the author, the tutor, or even Dr McDowell the Junior Dean, is an insignificant figure, but the man towers over his functions, functions which might be performed by a mere mortal. But Dr McDowell the man, the character, that superb artistic creation, where may his equal be found? Not in Oxford or Cambridge, certainly; only, perhaps, in the pages of Lewis Carroll, could he find a worthy peer. TRINITY NEWS 22.5.58

RB is clearly in a serious and honourable tradition of courageous

individualists partly unaware of, and partly unconcerned by, the amusement of lesser mortals. We came to realize that his work left little room for reflection on his appearance, or for any other aspect of social convention – it was not that he rebelled against pompous or pretentious rules (yes, found even in Trinity), but ignored them, except for outspoken comment, intended to be private. I think that it was his love, and mastery, of rapid, witty conversation which beguiled him to frequent attendance at student parties and meetings – plus, I feel, an element of vanity easily understandable, in the context of universal enjoyment of his company.
JOSEPH GOY (1953)

Like him, of course, there were some other great characters wandering around Trinity in the 1950s.
PATRICK MacDONNELL (1956)

The stories about McDowell are endless! In my opinion, he is a character of the eighteenth century, rather than the twentieth.
STERLING LACY (1973)

So I was told … the JD was walking across Front Square in the rain, reading a book, with a furled umbrella held aloft in his other hand.
CANON PETER NORTON (1961)

I heard that he was much delayed on a journey from Dublin to London, because he was carrying a toaster so ancient that it was suspected of being a bomb! YVONNE WATSON (1950)

I'd like to share a picture of my tutor answering my early morning knock on his door, eating a piece of toast and marmalade upside down! Even with marmalade on his chin, he gave just as good advice as ever and he seemed quite unaware of his appearance, as usual.
BEULAH BESHARAH (MCCABE) (1957)

I do recollect his habit of putting his hat on, as he emerged from his rooms or the Reading Room and then, realizing that it was back to front, twisting it round, still upon his head, as he crossed Front Square, looking for someone to talk to!

Roland Seaman, with whom I shared rooms in Botany Bay, told me that, as Auditor of the 'Theo' he did once ask Dr McD for some article, which, when completed, RB found under his bed! MALCOLM BOYDEN (1959)

To most of us around College, Dr RB McDowell is a curiosity – an institution to be pointed out to friends, relations and visitors, a kind of Trinity masterpiece, a relic from an antique past. True enough, he is a quaint character, but as with most curiosities, a little time spent on research notes proves to be valuable. And to those who have bothered to listen to his more than fluent flow of brilliant conversation, he emerges as a truly remarkable character.

But, to most, he remains an institution, a respected and valued one. His fantastic preoccupation with himself and his mind leads him to neglect the more conventional aspects of the self and so he appears to most as a badly dressed, slightly fey, oddity, which is far from the truth. TRINITY NEWS (1962)

He was very well-known of course, always featuring in *Trinity News* and universally imitated. At the time, I think that we suspected that much of the eccentric persona was deliberate, or deliberately exaggerated. Of course, we knew about such things – undergraduates know everything! GRAHAM WHEELER (1961)

His dignity isn't too fragile or he wouldn't do things for fun, like coxing a four down the Liffey at Trinity Regatta, or travelling to Italy in a motorbike sidecar. HENRY CLARK (1950)

Unfortunately, as I did a 'boat-train' degree – only turning up to take exams once or twice a year – my acquaintance with him was minimal, though memorable. Before meeting him, I had gathered that here was an eccentric and on visiting him in his rooms and seeing his rather unique filing system, I began to understand! TED COTHEY (1958)

SIGHTINGS IN FRONT SQUARE AND BEYOND...

One often saw the familiar figure of the Junior Dean, almost gliding, with characteristic short steps, across Front Square. Yet sometimes the figure would stop suddenly and multiple pockets would be checked, clearly with increasing consternation. Then, the figure would set off again, at great speed and with wide steps, in another direction. On these occasions, his overcoat and scarf would also momentarily fly up, as if taking off. The photograph is taken just after that stage. (See page 18.) Pity that I never got another at the exact earlier stage, which only lasted a moment.

CHRIS JOHNSTON (1966)

When I first came to Trinity, in 1948 my cousin, Owen McCarthy, pointed out RB to me, saying, 'He's a real character – just watch him. He is like Rikki-tikki-tavi (sic). He never crosses the middle of the Square, but always goes around by the walls, like Kipling's mongoose!'

DR CHRISTOPHER PETIT (1956)

I can remember him clearly, the caped character of Front Square!

JOHN TYLER (1964)

This actually happened ... I had rooms in 9RRG from 1957 to 1958, with the late Dave Pearson (who was killed some years later, driving a racing car). The JD was our neighbour, living in 9RFG. One damp evening, Dave and I were standing on the front doorstep, around 11 p.m., and Dave was eating a slice of bread and jam. The JD came in and we fell into conversation. 'Let's go over and talk on the Chapel steps, it's not raining over there,' said the JD.

CANON PETER NORTON (1961)

Specific stories are hard to recall. It was more the presence, and the coat, hat and scarf, that come clearly to mind, together with the erratic process across Front Square and conversations both with passers-by and with himself. ROGER KYNASTON (1966)

I think that it is important to emphasize that the JD had a tendency to walk backwards, scarf flapping, while talking to no-one .... which

I recall him doing in Front Square, after I gave him a Mars Bar that I'd received in a care package from my mother.
HEATHER O'BRIEN (LASKY) (1961)

I remember Dr McDowell often walking up and down Grafton Street, always wearing his hat and talking, talking, talking. He was well-known. LORD MEREWORTH (THE HON. DOMINICK BROWNE) (1950)

He talks as he walks. The policeman who used to control traffic at Front Gate always stopped everything immediately he saw the muttering, bespectacled, dark figure approaching.
TRINITY NEWS 23.2.61

I was doing Mathematics and, as a woman student, I came under the guidance of Miss Godfrey. So, my recollections are simply of him scurrying round Front Square like the White Rabbit.
MAUREEN MILLER (1953)

The JD was a compulsive newspaper reader. He would buy a selection of the evening or morning papers and spread them out on the floor of his living-room, crawling from one to the other, to compare their coverage of a particular story. His skip would pick them up regularly and discard them, enabling him to clean the carpet and to make room for a new intake of newsprint.
CANON PETER NORTON (1961)

Caro MacDonagh (1966), daughter of Patrick MacDonagh, the poet, told me that she, on occasion, observed RB taking circuitous routes to post letters around College Green – she believed that it was to make the whole thing interesting.
PETER IRONS (1966)

At a graduates' reunion dinner in the old (pre-fire) Dining-Hall, while we were feasting off the rarest of roast beef, McDowell insisted on being served a ham salad. EDGAR BRENNAN (1948)

McDowell's hat removed as a tease, 1969. Eoin 'The Pope' O'Mahony, Mariga Guinness and RB, well-layered. Photo copyright Patrick Guinness.

Recently, Ulick O'Connor, a man of letters and a barrister, published a diary. In it, he refers to Eoin O'Mahony and myself meeting over a meal and talking competitively. O'Mahony was a legendary figure and I heard, and must often have repeated, stories about him, but my contacts with him were infrequent, casual and short.

I should add that I once met him on the doorstep of a house and he borrowed his bus fare to Dublin. I maliciously thought that I would never see the money again, but O'Mahony went to considerable trouble to find me and repay the loan.
RB McDOWELL

When RB was living in New Square, I believe the students in the rooms below were puzzled by a mysterious mark appearing on their ceiling. On investigation, they discovered that the don, after showering, or, rather, washing in a tub, would step out and turn the tub upside down, to dispose of the water, presumably upon his uncarpeted floor! MALCOLM BOYDEN (1959)

As with others, I was intrigued by his eccentricities, even by the way that he negotiated crossing Front Square. My wife worked for a short while in Captain Shaw's office, in the early 1950s. She tells how, when he came to the office to have letters typed, he was always offered the customary cup of coffee, but that the biscuit box was hidden, if possible, and that if he left his scarf behind, there was the problem of how to handle it safely! THE VEN. HERBIE STUART (1948)

The Professor was rumoured to have tried to shoot duck during season, in the area of the cricket square. SAM DARBY (1975)

I used to use the Manuscripts Room (the 'Ivory Tower,' we called it) to read Old French texts. There, I witnessed at first hand Dr McDowell's habit of shredding paper into small bits as he read, leaving a small pile on the floor under his desk. I am glad to hear that he is still going strong, I hope. Although I do not believe that I ever met him directly, he was, to me, at least, a cheerful presence around Campus. AILEEN DENNE-BOLTON (1982)

It is alleged that, on going to North America, RB enquired about postage; he had heard that launderettes were cheaper there than in Dublin and he was planning to send all of his laundry to be cleaned in New York. ANON.

At table, his flow of incisive and never repetitive information and opinion sometimes included particles of food, most amusing to myself and my sister when we were children. He had an aversion to cats, of which my mother was fond – on their unwanted approach, he would call out, in his Belfast burr, 'Poo-sy, Poo-sy,' in pretended

McDowell makes a point, *c.* 1968. Photo copyright, Patrick Guinness.

friendship. In the strange world of adults, he was in a class of his own. PATRICK GUINNESS (1980)

With the passing years, McDowell's abilities, rather than his eccentricities, seem to be more clear in my mind.
DR KATHLEEN WELLS (MacLARNON) (1950)

RACONTEUR AND WIT

*O*nly *the unwary tackle Dr McDowell head-on. At his 80th birthday party, a graduate was heard complaining to him that, as Junior Dean, he had fined too many people, to which Dr McD replied, sharply, 'I should have fined faar more!'* A.L.

McDowell likes to talk a lot and, while he talks extremely well when his mind is fully engaged, he can run on a lot when his mind is elsewhere. One subject on which he is – or was – inclined to run on, is the Anglican liturgy. Once, I thought that it might be rewarding to interrupt him and it was.

'Tell me, McDowell,' I said, 'do you ever pray?'

'Prey?' he replied. In my memory, I can hear the 'e'. 'Only on the defenceless.'
DR CONOR CRUISE O'BRIEN (1940)

My grandfather, Dr Richard R. Leeper, was the Medical Superintendent of Swift's Hospital, St Patrick's ('He gave the little wealth he had, / To build a House for Fools and Mad: / And shew'd by one satyric touch, / No nation wanted it so much'.) He was a notorious raconteur and storyteller and his tour of the many Swift relics that he had collected was an impressive performance. RBMcD was keen to meet him and I arranged a dinner at St Patrick's Hospital, where the two had a fantastic raconteurs' duel, both very keen to get their stories across. Afterwards, my grandfather said to me, in fury, 'Who was that terrible show-off you brought? He never stopped talking!' (Takes one to know one!)
DR RICHARD MCCLELLAND (1943)

In about 1938 or so, when I was about nineteen and he, then as now, was some seven years my senior, he came to dinner at my family house, in University Square, Belfast. He talked very loudly and rapidly (and, of course, very interestingly) for the entire evening. When he had gone, my father, who was a doctor, said, 'That young man will not live long; he will have burnt himself out in a very few years.' My father, who spoke moderately and not very loudly, lived to be eighty.
MAURICE CRAIG (1944)

My father-in-law, Dr Tony Werner, was a lecturer in Chemistry in Trinity in the forties and fifties (his father, Emil Werner, was Professor of Chemistry for many years). Tony is now nearly ninety-two. He recalls that the joke then was:
Q: 'What is the definition of a monologue?'
A: 'A conversation between McDowell and Rowe!'
Rowe was the maths professor at the time – a very silent individual.
DR THOMAS ROSS (1963)

I was researching in the Long Room of the Library, when Professor O'Meara of the Medical School was showing the building to a colleague from Malaysia. In 'shimmered' (a Wodehouse word) RB, which led O'Meara to say, 'Here is the expert, my friend, Dr McDowell!' There came a disquisition on Malaysia. One who figured, was a Governor who came from a noble Trinity family. RB said that he had died of a very distressing cancer. O'Meara pressed for detail. RB eventually said, 'Cancer of the tongue.' O'Meara replied, 'I can see you would regard that as particularly distressing!' RB's answer was, 'Oh, very neat, O'Meara!'   FLORRIE O'DONOGHUE

The most incredible facet of the Junior Dean is his mind. This is not a joke. I spent several illuminating hours with him, one evening, drinking mulled wine (carefully brewed by mine host in a kettle) and I discovered that there is very little that he doesn't know. His knowledge of history is well-known, but not so is his insight into what goes on in College, which is quite frightening. And, besides being a good talker, he is an intelligent listener and, unlike most geniuses, he is eager to learn and find out things from his fellow conversationalists. True enough, sometimes you have to shout him down to get a word in edge-ways, but once that initial barrier is down, the rest is far from silence. TRINITY NEWS (1962)

RB himself has a host of good anecdotes worth recording, which he tells rather well. One that I remember is about having dinner in the old Dolphin Grill Room, some time in the war years '39–'45. A man, obviously home on leave from the war, leapt up from his table and hailed an old friend at the far side of the room. 'My goodness, Bill, what luck that we both had leave at the same time,' he said. 'We must have a round of golf this week.' To which the friend rather grumpily replied, 'I'd love a game of golf, but I'm not home on leave. I still just work for Guinness's!' A quick view of the tension between those who felt that they must go and fight in 1939 and those who didn't!

Another story was about talking in the 1930s to Robert Barton, the member of the County Kildare family who owned the famous chateaux in Bordeaux. He was, I presume, a Protestant Home Ruler and cousin of Erskine Childers, who had switched to Sinn Fein after 1918 and who was picked for Michael Collins's team, who went to London to negotiate the Treaty with Lloyd George, in 1921. He lived on, amazingly, until 1975. RB had asked him about Sir Roger Case-ment. Barton replied, 'Thank goodness I had very little to do with that disgraceful man! Do you realize that Casement went round Pris-oner of War camps in Germany in 1915, trying to persuade decent men from Irish regiments to fight for the Germans?' An interesting sidelight on degrees of republican sentiment, when the Free State was being created. HENRY CLARK (1950)

The JD was a superb raconteur. He talked faster than anybody else I had ever met and would illustrate his theme with numerous *excursi*, always returning to the main thread where he left off; after a few more words, he would branch off again. He could keep this going for many minutes and it was impossible to get a word in edgeways, even had you wished to do so. CANON PETER NORTON (1961)

We all remember RB as a great socialite. There was rarely a party in College in my time, in the fifties, which did not find him surrounded by a group, listening eagerly to his reflections on the human condition, in some form or another. Two such come to mind.

'I was in Westminster Abbey the other day, when I was approached by a darky (not that I would cast aspersions on our coloured brethren). He asked me, "Do you mean to say that there is one person buried under each of these tombs?" I said that I thought that was r-roughly the r-ratio.'

On another occasion, he was in combative conversation with Professor David Green of the Irish Language Department: 'While I can be confident that some of my students will in future be involved in the affairs of the great nations of the world, the most you can ever hope for is to be quoted in a footnote in a book on Middle Irish!'
REV. TOM ROBINSON (1955)

He was a great wit, but Hugh Gibbons, a great wit too, once matched him in a history lecture, after the JD had announced that Henry VIII had built a maze at Hampton Court for his amusement and Hugh replied, 'No, Sir, it was for his amazement!'
DOONIE SWALES (TOWNSEND) (1963)

He had a habit of prefacing remarks in conversation with, 'Speaking from memory,' (as though everyone else came around with a battery of works of reference). And I remember him once declaring on High Table on Commons that he'd been reading the *Koran*. 'It's rather like *Mein Kampf.*' Taking this to be a witty sally and, anyhow, amused by it, I ventured to laugh. 'Have you read it, Rogers?' I admitted that I hadn't. 'Then you shouldn't laugh!' DANIEL ROGERS (1954)

In my experience, stories that are funny when told mimicking voice and posture often fall somewhat flat, when put onto the written page. I am afraid that even one story from me about McDowell may demonstrate that. However, it has remained in my mind as a sort of classic TCD scene. A census was held in, I think, 1961. The Junior Dean was responsible for ensuring that all students in College that evening completed and submitted their census forms. I was deputed to help the JD and so, led by the Chief Steward with his lantern, McDowell and I, in our gowns, processed across Front Square to the lobby of the Dining Hall, where a table had been set up for the collection of the census forms.

I suppose that there were several hundred men to be checked. McDowell insisted on a quick review of each form, to make sure that it had been completed legibly and, I suppose, without profanity or levity. He paused at one offering and said, pointing at the box that required 'Religion' to be filled in, 'What's this, what's this? "Lapsed Catholic"? The officials don't want to have your spiritual odyssey, young man, they want to know what you are now.'
PROFESSOR ALAN TAIT (1962)

I had been away from College for some months. On my return, having to climb over a wall through a builder's yard at the back, I put my foot in a mixture of mortar. A couple of days later, meeting RB and being greeted with the words, 'I hear you are back making your impression!' JOHN PEARSON (1956)

Brian Boydell and RB were close friends for well over half a century. Brian borrowed the Junior Dean's office one evening, when the conductor of a visiting orchestra refused to change into his dress suit in the company of mere musicians. RB decided to do some work in his Junior Dean's office and found the sartorial conductor in proprietorial mode in his office. The following dialogue ensued:
    'Who are you?' enquired RB.
    'I'm the conductor.'
    'What route?'
DR SEAN BARRETT (JUNIOR DEAN 1986-2000)

This true story was at the reception in the Provost's House during the Hist's bicentenary (I was Censor that year). Ted Kennedy had made his televised speech in the Examination Hall and at the reception, when a group of us in gowns were standing around chatting with Joan Kennedy (his first wife), she asked us why we were on the platform and she was not. RB, who was standing next to us, replied, 'Madam, it is a simple case of having been around for four hundred years.' PATRICK O'SULLIVAN (1971)

HOUSE GUEST

Staying in a freezing bedroom at Leixlip in the sixties, RB groped about for his hat and coat for warmth and dragged up a Union Jack to his chin, thinking it was a bed cover. When he awoke in daylight and saw that he was draped in a flag, he knew he must be dead and promptly went to sleep again.
THE HON. DESMOND GUINNESS

He is the source and subject of endless stories. I have none of my own, but I would like to refer to one which you have no doubt heard from several quarters, namely the one when he woke up one morning in the attic at Leixlip Castle covered by the Union Jack, he said that he thought at first that he was dead on the field of honour. The point that I want to make is that the Union Jack must have been put on him by my sister-in-law, Mariga, as a comment or a tease, rather than to keep him warm – a flag is no eiderdown. His return comment was worthy of him; in fact the exchange was typical of them both.
LORD MOYNE (THE HON. JONATHAN GUINNESS)

He does love the country-house circuit. I've met him weekending with Dermot and Tiggy McGillycuddy at Bishops Court, at Leslie Hill, at Prehen House in Derry with the Pecks, and at Desmond and Mariga Guinness's parties, seeming very much at home with all the other guests. He's probably stayed at Birr Castle, Mount Stewart and Mount Juliet, too. He came up to County Derry to a dance at my home in January 1951 and was a great success. 'As good as a cabaret,' someone said, talking to everyone who wasn't dancing and getting on well with my mother. HENRY CLARK (1950)

RB now comes to stay with us about three times a year, including Christmas. He has become fond of our four cocker spaniels and we

are now on our fourth generation. They also look forward to his visits, particularly at mealtimes. At breakfast, while he is having his meal
at the counter, they are sitting underneath, to get their share – this, in
fact, happens at every meal! SIMON NEWMAN (1969)

The Perfect Guest. One weekend, some Trinity friends – and their
friends – descended upon our windmill in Surrey, for a long weekend.
A quantity of food and drink was laid in, the first testing of which
was at dinner on Friday. On Saturday morning some of us announced
that we were going beagling, then others were persuaded to join in,
until only one person preferred to remain in until we returned – this
was Dr McDowell. I pointed out interesting books, putting some
within range and recommending others. Everyone was sure (wrongly)
that several others had pointed out where the food was – in the
adjoining granary.

The beagling included drinking (there was no cruelty to animals,
as they never caught any – perhaps because hares don't go into pubs)
and, on our return, I was horrified to find that Dr McDowell had not
found the food! He assured us that he had had enough, as he had discovered a Stilton cheese and a loaf of bread on the sideboard. There
was a tiny hole and a little tunnel in both, such as a mouse would
make. Obviously, he did not wish to cause any trouble. He was the
perfect guest, and assured me that he had found my books most interesting. JILL MCEVEDY (1961)

Over the years, he has stayed with me both at my house in Ireland,
Port Hall, County Donegal, and in Greece, on the island of Euboia,
where for many years I rented a house each summer. At both, he
would arrive in tweed winter suit, battered pork-pie hat and warmly
dressed, with a heavy scarf, winter and summer alike. His first words
to my wife, Gina, were, 'Do you think you can shut that window –
there is a bit of a draught?' An ideal guest, always happy deep in an
armchair with a book, provided that no window was open. Always
knowledgeable and ready to discuss any subject.
ANTHONY MARECCO

GUEST

A FRIENDLY VISIT

When I was a little boy, in the 1950s, we lived in Cashel, County Tipperary, where my father was the local Church of Ireland Dean. The enormous deanery in which he was billeted was one of the few remaining Queen Anne residences in the twenty-six counties, lying in the shadow of the old Cathedral on the Rock behind the town. Today the luxurious Cashel Palace Hotel, it was then a crumbling pile, with a leaking roof and vast, seemingly unheatable, rooms. But it must have been architecturally interesting, as sometimes coaches full of Americans with Desmond Guinness would turn up to 'look at the architraves,' as we called it. I enjoyed conducting them upstairs to show off what, I proudly assured them, was the oldest flushing toilet in the country.

One morning, the doorbell rang. Mary, our occasional cleaning lady, threw down her duster and went to open the door. There, she found two individuals conducting an animated, but entirely incomprehensible, conversation. Ignoring completely her polite inquiry as to the nature of their business, the smaller of the two men suddenly seized his friend by the arm and shot past Mary into the house, still gabbling away at top speed. He began waving his arms around wildly and rushing from room to room, his companion in hot pursuit.

Mary panicked. She took to her heels and ran off into the depths of the house, yelling, 'Dean Jackson, Dean Jackson, where are you, come quick!' By the time she found my father, she was red in the face and could hardly speak. 'Your Reverence,' she gasped, 'come quick. There's some foreign madman after getting into the house and he's going to break everything up!' And that is why, one morning in 1958, although they were old friends from Trinity days, the Dean of Cashel welcomed Professor RB McDowell to his home, by charging at him with a brass poker quivering in his hand.

JOHN WYSE JACKSON

Whilst I was at Trinity, and as Secretary of DUCAC, obviously I was heavily involved with Trinity Week. I remember the first event of the week was the regatta and we had some American friends staying with us for the week and somewhat naturally they met RB at the regatta. They were so fascinated by him that my father invited RB to join us for dinner, at home at Dundrum on the following Tuesday. First of all, he took the wrong bus and was half an hour late and, because of his explanations, it took us a long time to introduce him to the other guests. In the fullness of time, around midnight, I drove him back to College and he let himself in by the side door. I went in as well, to watch him get safely back to his rooms.

He had, incidentally, during the course of the evening, promised to show the Americans around the Examination Hall, the Dining-Hall and the Chapel. On Trinity Wednesday we were strolling across Front Square, i.e. my parents, the Americans and myself, when my father saw RB and went over to tap him on the shoulder, whereupon he turned around and said, 'I know I have seen you somewhere but I cannot remember where!' which left my father speechless! RB felt very embarrassed when he realized and then, as he had promised, he showed the Americans around. SIMON NEWMAN (1969)

One day, RB came to lunch at an elegant address south of Dublin, where the hostess was unaware that he had been regaled elsewhere, the previous evening. He declined the soup politely, but agreed to nibble a piece of dry toast. He could not manage the main course, but, to spare the lady's feelings he said, 'However, I should like another slice of that delicious dry toast!' A third, very small, piece of toast did for pudding. PROFESSOR NIALL RUDD (1950)

I first met him as a child, in the 1960s, when he was a guest at my parents' house near Dublin, at lunch or supper. I recall him reacting to Mick Jagger, then the epitome of revolt, as a 'monkey fellow', which was exactly Jagger's physical appearance. I didn't realize that, as Dean of Discipline at TCD, RB probably felt that Jagger was a bad influence on students in general. His view moderated when he realized that MJ was quite well-read. PATRICK GUINNESS (1980)

My own most incongruous meeting with RB was certainly in Horse

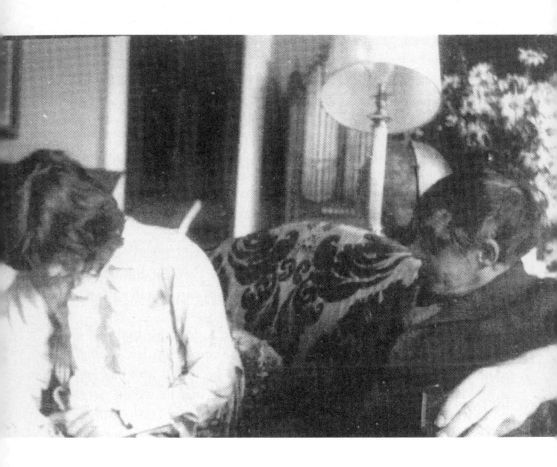

Mick Jagger with frilly shirt, RB with overcoat, 1967.
Photo copyright, Patrick Guinness.

Show Week, 1968, at the University (now Kildare Street) Club. He was coming out of the dining room with two, immediately recognizable, lunch guests. 'Oh, Henry,' he said, in his grandest voice, 'may I introduce you to Mr Jagger and Miss Faithful?' Marianne Faithful was Mick Jagger's steady partner in that year. RB had apparently met them at Leixlip with the Guinness's and had offered to show them the Book of Kells and give them lunch. He'd clearly kept them amused. HENRY CLARK (1950)

WEDDING GUEST

Here is my recollection of the time the JD attended my wedding in London, in June 1968. The reception was in the English Speaking Union in Charles Street and, though Dr McDowell had been asked, he had not been at the church and I did not expect him to attend. Then, as the reception was well under way, the familiar figure of the JD appeared at the door and, seeing him, I decided to ask him to make one of the speeches.

He was dressed in a somewhat crumpled suit, which had obviously seen better days. He said that he would make a speech, but that he must first change into another suit, which he was carrying in a brown paper parcel. I directed him to the Gents, downstairs.

Later, when he had not reappeared, I went to look for him and it sounded as if he was changing in one of the small cubicles. At that moment a Trinity friend, who was a wedding guest and who had evidently had quite a bit to drink, came in. I said that he would never guess who was in the locked stall. I said, 'It's the Junior Dean.' A look of sheer disbelief crossed my friend's face and he went at once and hammered on the door, shouting, 'McDowell, McDowell – come out of there and fight me!' 'Oh, my goodness,' said the JD within, 'who on earth is that and what in heaven's name is going on?' I'm not sure who was the most surprised when the cubicle door was opened. In any case, the Junior Dean, now wearing a suit only slightly less battered than the one in which he had arrived, made an excellent speech which was greeted by tumultuous applause.

His opening words were that he was totally perplexed that he, an

'The JD making a speech at my wedding. On the left is my father.'
PHOTO: GEORGE WINGFIELD (1968)

unmarried man in his middle fifties, should be asked to speak on the subject of matrimony! Of course, this was not the only time that he was required to expatiate on this tricky subject. (See page 78.)

GEORGE WINGFIELD (1968)

TV AND RADIO GUEST

NATIONWIDE RECOGNITION FOR THE JD

To watch television entails a sacrifice for undergraduates – borrow money for a few bottles in a bar, or freeze outside a plate-glass window in Grafton Street. But it is worth everyone's while to make the effort at 7.15 on a Tuesday night, when Telefís Éireann presents 'Postbag,' a discussion programme featuring Dr RB McDowell as a member of its distinguished panel.

In company with a school-teacher, a trade union official and a beauty expert, the Junior Dean considers questions sent in by viewers from all over Ireland, on all kinds of topics. He emerges as a polished and very engaging performer. The material, as always in such programmes, often descends to unbelievable fatuity and even a boundlessly inventive wit would be hard pressed to keep the show entertaining. But the panel cope nobly with such questions as the favouritism shown to male customers by waitresses and, given a chance, a real and vigorous discussion can develop. The Tuesday before last, for instance, a question on compulsory Irish found Dr McDowell in a long redoubt of dissent, standing out like a healthy thumb, as he refused to pay lip-service to the myth of 'The National Language'.

Should you watch the show, do not be deceived by appearances. The Junior Dean's sartorial elegance before the cameras does not mean conformity, or any diminution of that individuality with which Trinity has been familiar for so long and which Telefís Éireann is now presenting to the nation.

TRINITY NEWS 1.2.62

When giving a series of talks on Irish history for Ulster Television, RB turned up in his normal attire. They got a suit for him and at the end of the programme, he went off with it still on. A second time, they produced another suit and he went off wearing this one, too. On the third occasion, someone was delegated the job of seeing that McDowell did not leave the studio with the latest suit.

ANON.

During an Irish radio programme, someone raised the subject of marriage and at once the compère said, 'Well, I think that this is definitely one for you, Dr McDowell.' 'Well, yes, since I'm not one to suffer from this singular state!' began the JD.

Another time, when discussing on radio whether wolves in Ireland had died out at the end of the eighteenth century, the JD observed, quizzically, 'Who is to say that there is not one last wolf baying at the moon in County Roscommon?' Of course, all of these tales need to be retold in the JD's inimitable accent.

DOUGLAS WRIGHT (1968)

I heard him once on the radio, on LBC, while I was driving to work, and the interviewer asked him was it true that if you went to Oxford or Cambridge, that you had to do a dissertation, whereas, at Trinity College Dublin, you simply had to pay £20. McDowell's voice came back, as follows, 'Anyone who has had the benefit of a Trinity education can go out into the world and earn £20 and deserves an MA.'

DAVID DONNOLLY (1971)

In the early days of RTÉ Television, there was a panel programme of four, one of whom was RB. Viewers wrote in with questions: 'What does the panel think? What does the panel do?' etc. One question was, 'What do members of the panel do when they meet someone, recognise the face but can't put a name on him or her?' When it came to RB's turn, he said, 'This is always happening to me. I have a perfect answer for anyone over forty-five years of age – you simply ask, "How is the old complaint?" Everyone over forty-five has a complaint and they are delighted you remember it!'

DR RAYMOND REES (1944)

HOST

'I'm a natural guest, not a natural host.'
RB's reply on behalf of the guests at the Old Campbellians' dinner at
the Kildare Street and University Club.
DR SEAN BARRETT, DEPT OF ECONOMICS, TCD

In those days he lived on the ground floor in No. 8 on Front Square,
cared for by Larry, one of the best of the skips. For several years, he
had piles of pictures leaning against the wall, which just never got
hung up. He's always suffered from the cold and his bed was a deep
pile of blankets and coats. HENRY CLARK (1950)

To be avoided at all costs, was an invitation to his rooms for sherry
and sandwiches. Whatever about the former, the latter were usually
two weeks old, having been made by his mother in Belfast, for his
train trip to Dublin.

If this all sounds somewhat negative, it is not intended, for his company was most enjoyable. ALAN COOK (1955)

Visiting his rooms for a tutorial, I remember books piled everywhere,
the remnants of the odd meal yet to be tidied away, coffee cups all
over the floor and nowhere to sit!
ROGER KYNASTON (1966)

There was the apocryphal story about his mother coming down to
Dublin once a term, to make sure that his rooms were clean and tidy.
From what I remember of his rooms, they certainly were littered –
books everywhere, on the floor, under chairs and on chairs. But
what's wrong with that? I always found him a reasonable chap to deal
with and tolerant of undergraduate foible – usually in the matter of
explaining why I had missed Night Roll yet again.
LT.-COL. ROBIN ANDERSON (1961)

Occasionally, he invited two or three of us to his rooms for sherry or
cocoa, to continue some lengthy conversation. I recall a living-room

resembling an igloo built of books, including so many on the floor that there was hardly room to get to the broken armchairs. He had his favourites among the more aristocratic undergraduates from all of the faculties, including my physicist friend Malcolm McCausland, from whom I heard many priceless anecdotes, now sadly forgotten. It was clearly unnecessary to be reading history, to recognize a brilliant and hugely likeable personality. JOSEPH GOY (1953)

The other night, I was discussing Dr McDowell with a friend, a well-known medical student.

'I regard,' I said, 'that super-human and god-like being with awe; to me, he is quite perfect!'

'But what an absurd thing to say,' replied Paddy, 'about a man who waters his claret!'

For a moment, I was stunned by the enormity of the accusation, then I sprang to his defence.

'If,' said I, fixing him with a severe glance, 'what you say were true, it might detract from the character of Dr McDowell as a host, but it cannot detract from the stature of Dr McDowell the man.' TRINITY NEWS 22.5.58

A brace of stories were told to me by my daughter recently and she, Nicola Lush-McCrum, is a TCD graduate, as am I. This story concerns Mike (MR) Beamish (1981), who was in the Ist XI Cricket Team, in fact I think that he was Captain of the XI at the time. He is a friend of mine, since I taught him at St Columba's College. Mike was invited by RB up to his rooms for sherry, in the Trinity Term. On the appointed day, he very timidly presented himself at the door of RB's rooms, not knowing quite what to expect from this strange eccentric; the door opened and in a volley of words, Mike was invited in by RB. A glass was thrust into Mike's hands. It was just an ordinary tumbler and from a dusty sherry bottle some sherry was poured into the glass, about an inch deep. RB remarked, 'I have had this sherry a long time so it is well-matured and, as they say down here, "Slánchwe".' Mike raised his glass, had a look at the glass's contents and was horrified to see a dead bee reclining in the sherry. Having been brought up well in St Columba's, he bided his time and listened to RB discourse about the Moravians, until there was a knock on the door and two fair-haired, handsome young men came in. In the meanwhile, Mike disposed of the sherry into a pot containing some very dead roses and made his departure graciously, saying, 'I have to attend Cricket nets and thank you for such a pleasant interlude.' He left the bee in the tumbler.

NORMAN LUSH (1951) *&* NICOLA LUSH-MCCRUM (1982)

I remember the following amusing story, of being a guest of one of TCD's Great Eccentrics. One night in Trinity Term, 1960, just after the 1937 Reading Room had closed down, while making my way across Front Square to catch a bus to bring me home to Blackrock, I was hailed by the unmistakable figure of Dr McDowell, who invited me to his rooms for a glass of sherry. No doubt with non-stop, kindly enquiries about the state of my studies, while swinging his famous keys, he made his way to those hospitable chambers. A very dark room greeted me. My host bade me take a chair, while he proceeded to the wash basin, where he collected a plastic mug which contained a spare pair of false teeth. Ridding the mug of this encumbrance, McDowell filled it with sherry, handed it to me and then turned to find a vessel for his own libation. With understandable apprehension of what might be lurking in this mug, which had been in such close contact with lips accustomed to pour forth wisdom non-stop, I hastily poured the potion on the carpet and pretended to enjoy my offering from the Great Man, while I am sure I greatly enjoyed listening to his talk.   MORGAN DOCKRELL (1960)

I was invited to Dr McDowell's rooms one winter's evening, about 1960 – whether as thanks for inviting him to a boat club party, or to be admonished for some misdemeanour, I cannot recall. On knocking, I was invited to make my way between piles of papers and books that littered the floor, some thickly covered in dust, towards the turf fire blazing in the grate. He invited me to have a glass of mulled wine, which I gratefully accepted. Whereupon he filled a half-pint tankard with red wine, removed a red-hot poker from the fire, plunged it sizzling into the glass and passed the, now mulled, wine across. I enjoyed the charred wine and stimulating conversation that followed. GERRY BLANCHARD (1965)

I had acquired a certain notoriety for impersonating the Junior Dean, in numerous College Revues and Dublin cabarets; however, I didn't actually know whether or not he had ever seen my version, until the summer revue in my last year – when, during one performance I looked up and there, in the doorway at the back of Players Theatre, stood the unmistakable silhouette of Dr McDowell – rather like the figure of Salieri, when he appears as Mozart's father in *Amadeus*, actually. I seem to remember the sketch featured a professor in Irish History winning a talent competition by playing, 'Mamma Don't Allow No Key Playing Here' on a large bunch of keys...

Anyway, happily enough, he invited me back to his rooms afterwards for a drink, where for the next uncounted hours we sat drinking boiled wine, served direct from the kettle – at least I think that it was wine and I think that it was a kettle – and talking into the small hours. Or, rather, I sat listening while he wandered about talking – because as anyone who knows the man will be aware, there are very, very few subjects on which he is incapable of pronouncing. He has one of the most phenomenal mental ranges of anyone that you will ever meet and his retention of detail is quite staggering. By the end of the night, I was quietly hoping that he didn't know quite as much about me, as he did about my peers – although I'm pretty sure that he did.

As I left, my host finally wondered what I was going to do, once I had graduated. I replied that I was going to become an actor. He smiled, with what appeared to be great relief. 'Oh fank heavens for vat,' he sighed. 'Rumour had it vat you were finking of becoming an academic.'

He had no worries on 'vat' score. I might have been able to fit into his hat all right – but there was no way I would have been able to fill his shoes. TERENCE BRADY (1961)

In his rooms in the Rubrics, I would occasionally drink red wine with him into the wee small hours. He would talk incessantly, seldom drawing breath, so that it was difficult to get a word in edgeways. One sometimes succeeded though and, if done cleverly, one could steer the conversation in a different direction, to provide a bit of variety. In winter I remember sitting with him in this rather bare room, close to a small gasfire, which he would keep turning lower and lower, presumably for economy's sake. This meant that, to avoid the bitter cold, both of us had to advance our chairs closer and closer, until our knees were nearly touching, at which point I would complain and he would turn the fire up again, allowing one to withdraw somewhat.

GEORGE WINGFIELD (1968)

One warm July Saturday afternoon, in a deserted Front Square, I was engaged by the Junior Dean in a long discussion on the current military threat to peace. (It was 1961, too late for Suez and too early for the Falklands, but I cannot recall the exact crisis.) We parted after about twenty minutes and I felt a slight glow of pride that I, a Commerce undergraduate, should have been the one to be chosen, maybe accosted, for such a lengthy exchange. I went round to wheel my Lambretta out of the shelter, pushed it to the entrance of the GMB, heaved it onto its stand and ran up to a friend's bedsitter, to find out if he wanted a drink later. He would be revising – sensible chap. As I came out of the GMB, there was the Junior Dean, his hand on the seat of the Lambretta.

'This your scooter, Ridley?'

'Yes, Sir.'

'Ten shillin' fine. Ten shillin' fine. No parking at any time.'

I thought, 'You so and so! I spent twenty minutes being polite, there's hardly a soul in College, I leave my Lambretta for ninety seconds, I'm usually such a law-abiding type and you go and fine me!'

I went up to my rooms (above the coffee bar and beneath the Knights), made out my cheque for ten shillings and gave it to the Junior Dean. An hour or so later I returned, having established that there wasn't a girl left in Trinity Hall who wasn't revising, legally parked the Lambretta in the shelter and moodily slouched off to my rooms. A note was pinned to the door, summoning me to Dr McDowell's rooms. I went round. It was about 6.30 p.m.

The Junior Dean: 'Do you drink port, Ridley?'

'Well, yes, sir.'

'There's only one way to drink port, Ridley, and that is to drink the whole bottle between the two of us.' He had decanted the port, produced a loaf of bread and some cheese ... and I remember little else! DAVID RIDLEY (1964)

As a very new undergrad (Civil Engineering), I was approached by the JD to come out for a jar, one evening. I believe that he had taught at my (public) school at some period, but that was the only connection and I was questioning what this was all about. Anyway, we got into conversation – at least he did – over a stout for him and a cider for me and the bit that I recall ran something like this ... 'Well, now, there's a lot of different kinds of beer. Stout is a kind of beer and lager is another one and there's ale. But then there is cider ... now, I don't think you'd call that a beer.' TIM WILLCOCKS (1965)

I Remember the first lunch 'à deux' in his rooms in the Rubrics, on a cold wet day in 1981, with newspaper for a tablecloth, plenty of pâté, cheese, French bread and butter, ripe pears and meringues – his favourite foods – and champagne – which neither of us could open! So RB set off for assistance from Desmond, the wine waiter in the Dining Hall, champagne bottle under his coat, in the weather that he hates so much! A three hour lunch could happily have gone on longer, but for a pre-arranged meeting for the JD. He is such good company. JENNIFER LYONS (Mrs F.S.L. Lyons)

TOUR GUIDE

I remember that, towards the end of my time as a student – from 1947 to 1948 – he used to lead visits to places of interest, e.g. Dublin Castle, St Patrick's, etc., accompanied by a flood of anecdote, very much in the style later adopted by David Norris, in his 'Joyce Monologues'. ERIC EARLE (1948)

Dr McDowell conducted us on a tour of the Provost's House some years ago, at one of the reunions and he was most entertaining. He had already retired by that time, but came up for the day. It took me a while to realise that the people he was talking about so vividly, as if he had spoken to them only the previous week, had been dead for hundreds of years.   BILL HIPWELL (1959)

TOURIST ATTRACTION

DR MCDOWELL COMMENTS:

*A*bout twenty years ago, I was up one of the ladders in the Long Room, near the Book of Kells and the tourists were much more interested in watching me on the ladder, than they were in the Book of Kells!

A MAN TO RELY ON

During my first year as a PhD. student, when I had been strictly warned off too much extra-curricular activity, I nevertheless co-wrote, and appeared in, a Players' Review number called 'Helluva Hula' – grass skirt and nearly all. On the opening night, as the curtain went up, I was horrified to see my ex 'moral tutor', RB McDowell, sitting front row centre. Whether under the stress of emotion or not, at that juncture my bikini top burst off – but I don't think he so much as blinked.   DR JILL SHEPPARD (ROBBINS) (1957)

At Leixlip, 11 miles west of Dublin, my parents Desmond and Mariga Guinness always invited people with no close family at Christmas, and RB was a frequent guest in the 1960s. His aversion to turkey was well known – 'No, no thank you, I don't take birrrd' – and so some spiced beef was always prepared for him.

At Christmas in 1972 we were at Osbaston in Leicestershire, the guests of my uncle Jonathan, now Lord Moyne. RB was among a house party of about two dozen, with spiced beef doubtless on the menu.

Jonathan's late father-in-law, Mr Lisney, was a grumpy former RAF pilot, with strong views on race and the issue of immigration into England. He had even moved to Spain after the war and admired Franco's régime. He stood to toast our hosts at the end of dinner and added some of his opinions, something along the lines of, how nice it was to celebrate a typical English Christmas and to see a table with no black faces around it and how we should all strive to keep them out.

My father then stood to say that Christmas should be an inclusive time, regardless of the colour of one's skin, at which Mr Lisney left the room. I recall the sudden pride that I felt at this intervention. But, within about a minute, Mr Lisney returned with a levelled shotgun in his hands and walked slowly around the table towards my father. All talk ceased mid-sentence. RB stood up and held up his hands. 'Now, look here, put that thing down,' and took hold of the barrel – firmly but unhurriedly – pushing it away from the table. 'Is it loaded?' Mr Lisney said nothing and left the room with the gun, not to return.

It had been a silly bluff, but only RB had had the presence of mind to face the situation at once, despite being of slighter build than Mr Lisney. He had intervened quickly and diplomatically and had put himself in the way of possible harm. To my youthful mind, RB grew in stature from being a voluble, endearing eccentric, to someone who had also shown his true mettle. PATRICK GUINNESS (1980)

CLUB-MAN

When I was at Trinity, we formed a small dining club and McDowell was our first guest, speaking at the inaugural dinner, in May 1965. He subsequently became a member and he is always invited to our annual dinner in London; we meet at a different club each year, using a private dining room. One year, having said that he was coming, and having paid, he never turned up. It transpired that he had gone to the wrong London club and found another private function, which had nothing to do with Trinity. Not realizing his mistake, he joined the party, had an excellent dinner, entertained everyone there and was made entirely welcome, although nobody knew who he was (apart from very obviously being an Irish eccentric!). Their gain was very much our loss, particularly as I had to refund him the cost of his dinner with us. As an Ulsterman, he always was very canny about money. Incidentally, we still see him at our meetings and continue to enjoy his company hugely. CHRISTOPHER KNOX (1967)

'The Professor' has many incarnations and is much loved in many quarters. Not least in the Ben Nicolson/Philip Toynbee Lunch Club (BN, son of Harold and Vita Sackville West, art historian and PT, journalist, started lunching together in Fitzrovia, 50 years ago). The tradition endures and RB McD is part of it. He's been a member for years. It has, I think, played quite a major part in his London life. I often meet him there. We also lunch together (Garrick/Reform, or my flat) on other occasions. I am devoted to him. I like his brio (amongst other things). For one thing, how many people have two books (Wolfe Tone's *Letters* and *Grattan*) reviewed, in very complimentary terms, in their 90th year (see the *TLS* of some months ago)?

I would draw to your attention the following vignette. It captures the ethos of the club. I once found myself sitting between two men. Neither the man on my left nor the man on my right had (I think) the slightest idea who the other was. Nor would they normally have had anything to say to each other. In fact, we were all getting on famously. The man on my left was RB McD. The man on my right was George Melly. I couldn't make up my mind which was funnier – the idea that RB McD should have had the remotest interest in jazz, or that George Melly knew anything about Irish history.
ROBERT BAILEY-KING

RB is the consummate club-man. Our meetings, private and professional, are always in the Kildare Street and University Club at no. 17, St Stephen's Green, his home from home in Dublin, where he determines who's in, who's out. He presides in a corner of the upstairs bar, receiving and dispensing, across from the group portrait of distinguished fellow members where he features, quaffing sherry, scattering crisps, salting the air with pithy observation: the pedigree of one, the cultural leanings of another, the backstory to a news headline. He is at large in a post-imperial playpen, moving many-coloured blocks of unfaltering anecdote through the sandpits of Europe and farther afield: the David of Iraq, the Goliath of the Anglo-American alliance (to which he owes allegiance); his old pupil Nicholas Tolstoy *versus* Lord Aldington (divided loyalty there): relentlessly, effervescently *ad hominem*, a man amongst men. ANTONY FARRELL (1971)

Dr RB McDowell and Professor Herries-Davies leaving the Examination Hall on Trinity Monday, 2002.·

Academe

PUBLICATIONS

As Ireland's leading eighteenth-century historian, RB McDowell is the author of the following historical studies:

Irish Public Opinion 1750–1800 (1944), *British Conservatism 1832–1914* (1959), *The Irish Convention 1917–1918* (1970), *The Church of Ireland 1869–1969* (1975), *Ireland in the Age of Imperialism and Revolution 1760–1801* (1979), (with D.A. Webb) *Trinity College, Dublin 1592–1952: An Academic History* (1982), '*Land & Learning – Two Irish Clubs*' (1993), *The Fate of the Ulster Unionists* (1997), *Crisis and Decline: The Fate of the Southern Unionists* (1997), *Grattan: A Life* (2001); also essays in biography, *Alice Stopford-Green, A Passionate Historian* (1967) and (with W.B. Stanford) *Mahaffy, An Anglo-Irishman* (1971), and *Historical Essays 1931–2001: A McDowell Miscellany* (forthcoming 2004).

He is also at work on the correspondence of Edmund Burke.

MCDOWELL AT EIGHTY

DR DAVID DICKSON TALKS TO THE MOST ACTIVE AND PROLIFIC IRISH HISTORIAN OF HIS GENERATION

DD: *How important was family background and schooling in the development of your historical interests?*

R B M C D : I was born in the middle of the middle classes, so from the very earliest days I was aware of how the business world thought and lived. I also grew up in the Protestant world of the North of Ireland, not, so far as I was concerned, a particularly grim world. My father's business was largely with Catholics in the South and he developed many personal relationships with his customers. The atmosphere was fairly tolerant. As a matter of eccentricity in my later teens, I became rather fascinated by Catholicism, not specifically Irish Roman Catholicism, but Catholic philosophy and the Gothic churches. I read pamphlets of the Catholic Truth Society with gusto: I liked the dialectics and I liked ceremonial and, possibly, given a slight pressure I might have drifted, as some of my generation did, into Roman Catholicism. But what were much deeper, both emotionally and as strong moral and intellectual convictions, were my unionist feelings. Looking back, I am thankful that I grew up in an area and in a world which was proudly provincial. I am putting it bluntly – you were able to combine strong local attachments with cheerful, exhilarating and encouraging membership of a greater world. The context of my loyalties, my political ideas, my prejudices and way of life, became and remained the British Isles. I had very few nationalists to clash with in my youth, so I never had to express my unionism very energetically. But it was there, pretty deep-set.

D D : *Your school, the Royal Belfast Academical Institute, has also produced D.B. Quinn, J.C. Beckett and T.W. Moody – a remarkable run of Irish historians. How did it influence you?*

R B M C D : I had two superbly good history teachers. One was John Pyper, who was grey-looking, always wore a grey suit and had rather a grey face. He was a quiet man, but had a very strong intellect and a powerful personality. The other was Archie Douglas, who was exuberant and entertaining. Neither man had, I suspect, any theory of teaching. As far as I can remember, they talked and we talked with them and both were extremely widely-read. The school had a very good library and there was the Linen Hall down the street, so I had plenty of books at my disposal. At the age of fifteen I read almost the most stimulating thing that I have ever read, Macaulay's *Essays*. Suddenly, I saw the key to all eighteenth-century political history. I mentioned to a school-master that I was reading Macaulay and he said, 'Journalism, read Gibbon.' So I went off and read Gibbon. In my later schooldays, I read Carlyle (at seventeen, his *French Revolution* was wonderful and I was so impressed, that I ploughed, with intermittent pleasure through his *Frederick the Great* – I recommend it), Clarendon and Churchill's *World Crisis*, which had just come out. Going through the same mill at about the same time were Moody, Beckett and Quinn. We all knew one another at school, but our standings were different. Moody was at one end and I was at the other, but we did meet.

D D : *What of the history course that you took as an undergraduate?*

R B M C D : It consisted of what nowadays would be called great survey courses on European and British history, some economic history, which came up to about 1920 (political history stopped about 1900) and, what was highly stimulating, political science. By modern standards, it was rudimentary – no statistics, no computers, no models. It consisted of reading Hobbes, Locke, Machiavelli, Rousseau, J.S. Mill and Marx. There was only one special subject: The French Revolution. A modern undergraduate would probably think it rather spartan fare. As for teaching, you had lectures; that was all, practically. I read extremely widely and somewhat indiscriminately. There is a good side in that and a bad. You might find an unexpected highway, or get an unexpected insight. But you might also waste a lot of time. I read Lecky while I was working for Scholarship and was able to answer a whole question from my reading; I think that tipped the scales, so I have always had a particular veneration for Lecky. I read Froude at about the same time. People who really impressed me were Mill, Hobbes, Marx, Weber, Manheim and Spengler. I was given *Das Kapital* in my last year by Constantia Maxwell: I found the first few pages exasperating and came to the conclusion that they were wrongheaded, but for the rest I admired and enjoyed Marx as an economic historian. Like many at the time, I was influenced by the whole concept of the economic factor in history and was fascinated by class divisions.

DD: *How important was Moody's arrival?*

RB McD: Moody arrived as Professor in 1939 (I had already completed my PhD thesis). He was at least twenty years younger than his colleagues, Alison Phillips, Curtis and Maxwell. So he came of a new generation and his aims were to bring the course up to date, to allow a much wider variety of choice and a greater degree of specialization, closer contact between teacher and taught, to promote essay-writing and criticism and to encourage research. It was very much the programme of the day at all other British and Irish universities. It took time to implement; it was just beginning when I became a lecturer in 1945. Now, while I enjoyed teaching, I never had great interest in the techniques; I was prepared to fall in – in other words, I was a typical mercenary, who would use any weapon that was provided, or would fall into any form of military organization where my services would be of use. I thought on the whole that the changes were good but, now, my instinct might be to say, well, why not leave a bigger margin for individual time? One of his colleagues, a devoted medievalist, was resolutely opposed to a great many of Moody's suggestions, partly, I think, on principle. She had grown up in the generation where constitutional history was treated as the subject which gave stamina to 'ordinary' history; it resembled law, or even mathematics, in that you had to work at it, whereas the other things for her were rather flimsy. There were also considerable differences in temperament.

DD: *Had Moody a clear agenda for the development of history in Ireland?*

RB McD: I doubt if he had a consciously formed agenda, but he and Edwards, who co-operated with him in founding the Irish Historical Society and *Irish Historical Studies*, had both been research students at the *Institute of Historical Research* in the Pollard age — an era which fervently believed in the value and attainability of objectivity and which emphasised unflagging industry, precision and bibliographical thoroughness. *IHS* was very much Moody's creation. Its appearance and layout reflected his sensitive interest in typography and for nearly forty years as editor, he persuasively encouraged the authors of articles and reviewers to bring their contributions into line with his high standards. Also, when the number of research students in the TCD History Department multiplied – in my day I was the only post-graduate – Moody spent endless time and trouble as a supervisor of his students. However, I feel that it would be a mistake to assume that a revolution occurred in Irish history about 1940. After all, when the Irish Historical Society and *IHS* were launched, some of Moody's and Edward's contemporaries, competent historians, were already at work – not to speak of the older generation (Falkiner, who died tragically young, Eoin MacNeill, Orpen, Aubrey Gwynn and Curtis). What happened was an updating, not a revolution.

D D : *How would you characterize your own approach to the writing of history?*

R B M C D : A lot of people, including many of the people I know, would approach history in terms of questions and answers and of the possibility of revision, of revising a view. Influenced by the Carlyles and the Clarendons and by interesting novels, I have always seen a piece of historical work as painting a picture and describing it. I know it is perfectly easy to say: is there any difference, really, between answering a question and describing? A person with a good philosophical mind would possibly point out that you cannot describe without asking the question: what do you see? But there is a slight difference in approach. History to me is a grand Tolstoyan unrolling, rather than cold analysis.

D D : *Do you feel that the writing of history should be primarily for public consumption, something that reaches beyond the student and the specialist?*

R B M C D : Now I do not wish to appear a rogue elephant. I have always conformed outwardly to the rules of academic history and have never denied the fact that I am an academic man. With certain of my acquaintances, I would even stress that I am an academic historian compared to people, who are, to put it bluntly, journalists, with an eye not only on the public, but on their publishers' accounts – they want to see a good statement. They are not only trying to lead the public in the right way, but they want to make money. I feel that history should be addressed to what I would call the educated world. To me the educated person is not one who has necessarily got a university degree; he or she is a person who has usually gone to a decent school and has kept in touch with reasonably intelligent and active people throughout life. I use the word 'educated' to indicate the generally intelligent, alert, publicly aware individual – those are the sort of people you want to be read by. I rather shiver when I discover the kind of work where you feel the writer is almost deliberately shutting out the public and it is an esoteric game which I have seen practised at its best by philosophers. A word which Americans are fond of using, the guild, suggests craftsmen under control. I do not think Michelangelo or da Vinci belonged to guilds – they went off and did their work without much respect either for wage settlements or for anything else. There can be the danger of getting into a closed room, in which the experts chat to and fro and impinge very little on the outside world. I do not want to see history in that room.

DD: *Which of your own books do you look upon with the greatest satisfaction?*

RB McD: May I fall back on what Somerset Maugham said once, when he was asked to write a preface to one of his earlier novels? He said that he read it with great interest, but he scarcely remembered it, it was quite new to him. One forgets. I am always absorbed in the present and thinking about the future – except for professional reasons of course. I do not think a great deal about the past. I am unlikely to be turning over what very nice meetings I have had in Dublin this past fortnight or so; no, I am thinking about what I am going to do for the next week. I am a future thinker.

HISTORY IRELAND Winter 1993

HISTORIAN

He was, and is, a very distinguished historian, in the generation immediately following T.W. Moody and ... Roy Foster. A historian and a character; and, in top form, a marvellous speaker.
ERIC EARLE (1947)

Historian and Scholarly Giant: anyone disposed to read these legends should spend half an hour sampling the detailed, erudite but readable style of his historical writing – a monumental labour of love, meticulous, wise and supremely authoritative.
JOSEPH GOY (1953)

As an historian he 'probably knows more about late eighteenth-century Irish history than any man living,' according to the *Times Literary Supplement*. His interest in eighteenth-century Ireland and the Versailles Court of Louis XIV give an insight to his nature: he relishes the sense of intimacy, the gossip and high life, the close aristocratic flavour of those times. TRINITY NEWS 23.2.1961

I studied under McDowell approx. 1967-71. He is the world's best living source on Irish Georgian history, as you know. I had the pleasure of meeting him over a cup of tea recently, at the Kildare Street University Club. We talked about Edmund Burke. I had done a paper on Burke and had used some of McD's material. I am a PhD student in History at the Maxwell School at Syracuse University. I still have my notes on McD's lectures from thirty years ago here in New York, on Irish Radicalism, and I will be going through them. It was a great privilege for me to know McD. Sadly, I was too young to appreciate him. RONALD N.G. FERGUSON (1972)

I don't know particulars with other College academics, but feel that some attention might be given to that with Professor Edmund Curtis who, I believe, supervised his Doctoral Thesis and with whom he edited *Irish Historical Documents*, for many years a staple reference

Melissa Webb (Stanford), Dr RB McDowell and Danae O'Regan (Stanford), in Front Square, quartercentenary, 1992.

work. His many other publications earned him, I believe, an international scholastic reputation. PETER IRONS (1966)

I seem to remember a story about his producing a brilliant paper for his History Finals. Indeed, it was rumoured that he knew more than his preceptors. The only trouble was that the examiners could not read his handwriting and marked accordingly. But, given that he has been a member of the academic staff of Trinity, the story (if true) must have had a happy ending and again it is hard to comment on the accuracy of the story. LT.-COL. ROBIN ANDERSON (1961)

An aspect of him that I vaguely recall, and it may be totally apocryphal, is that he was required to go and read his final degree papers to the examiners, as his writing was too difficult to decipher. And the reason why I remember this is because this happened to my college 'wife' also, who had this precedent quoted to him.
ULRIC SPENCER (1951)

RB McDowell was a frequent visitor to the Stanford family home in Mount Salus, Dalkey. His lively presence, erudition and wit were greatly enjoyed by all the family. His collaboration with W.B. Stanford on *Mahaffy – An Anglo-Irishman* (1971) – if at times slightly fraught (due to their different personalities) – created a scholarly yet entertaining portrait of the famous former Provost, whose anecdotes, like those of another famous TCD graduate, Oscar Wilde, can happily still be heard reverberating around the Dining Hall and across Front Square.
MELISSA WEBB (STANFORD) (1965)

Latterly, I have met Professor McDowell at such places of resort as the Public Record Office and the Institute of Historical Research and I have come to appreciate the way in which vagueness of manner conceals an acute and practical mind, with such a lively interest in contemporary as well as historical affairs. In 1990, when our unscrupulous media were in hot pursuit of the notorious 'Fifth Man', a passing attempt was made to incriminate my relative, Professor C.D.

Broad, Fellow of Trinity College, Cambridge, who also held an honorary degree from TCD and who was, of course, conveniently dead. Encountering Professor McDowell in the London Library, he sympathised with me and was dismissive of the recent calumny, about which he had evidently kept himself informed. I feel that this continuing interest in others gives a true indication of his own lack of egocentricity. JENNIFER MILLER (HART) (1954)

In 1995 Dr McDowell gave me practical and worldly-wise advice, regarding the procedure for the adoption of the revised Constitution for the London Branch of the Trinity Association. I am glad to say that I followed his advice and the draft Constitution was adopted without controversy. JOHN KEETCH (1968)

Some years ago a Committee of the House of Lords heard a petition from the Irish Peers that their right to representation be restored. McDowell attended the public hearings; on leaving the Committee Room for a lunchtime adjournment, he almost tripped on a step, but was saved from falling by the intervention of a tail-coated attendant, who urged, 'Have a care, M'lord.'
DR R.A. SOMERVILLE (1972) Dept of Economics, TCD

There is a new *Dictionary of National Biography* under way. RB McD is, I think, particularly pleased at having been asked not only to nominate those Irishmen who got left out or who ought to have been included, but also to write some of the lines (or 'notices', as I believe they are called).
ROBERT BAILEY-KING

LECTURER AND TUTOR

McDowell and I were undergraduates at around the same time – he being a year ahead – and I got to know him quite well. We took long walks together, during which he, of course, did most of the talking, generally both entertainingly and instructively. After I had taken my first Moderatorship, in Modern Literature, I decided to take a Supplementary Moderatorship, in Modern History. McDowell kindly agreed to coach me. His coaching was severely practical; what sorts of questions were likely to come up and how to answer them effectively. As a result, almost entirely because of his coaching, my Supplementary Mod. was a First and led on to a PhD in Modern History, which has remained my primary interest ever since. So, I owe McDowell a great deal, as I know do many other people.
DR CONOR CRUISE O'BRIEN (1940)

In those days, it was a notable failing that few of the Trinity faculty socialized with students – or, as RB might have called us, undergraduates. At Cambridge, later, I found Fellows and lecturers much more approachable. At Trinity, RB was certainly the first lecturer most of us got to know well. HENRY CLARK (1950)

I recall a poem about the staff of the History faculty, published in TCD in 1947, '48 or '49, beginning:
'Though to sleep I'm driven by the drawl of Otway Ruthven,
Or the semi-nasal howel emitted by McDowell.'
THE REV. EDMUND RAINSBERRY (1948)

I found Irish history very boring, although Moody did his best to make it interesting. RB amused our year. Most thought that he was eccentric, some that he was quite mad. GERALD DRAPER (1946)

Some of us, especially those who missed National Service, took the History courses rather seriously and in our innocence stood in moderate awe of the magisterial Professor Moody, the droning Miss

Otway-Ruthven (-de-Burgh), the dapper F.S.L. Lyons, not to mention, the remote figure of Daddy Luce. RB presented a highly contrasting impression of cheerful enthusiasm, youthful energy, approachability and earnestness. The English contingent was amused by his high-pitched tones, further distorted by his obvious difficulty with the role of lecturer, especially outside his beloved period, eschewing the common practice of reading out the same chronological notes verbatim, every year. After many hilarious paper-shufflings, he would screech 'Now last day ... we...,' followed by phrases and paragraphs delivered in a mixture of speeds, ranging from a cawing one word per two seconds (but including endless interjections of 'um...um...um...,' to a startlingly high-pitched machine-gunning of about ten words per second. We knew from the latter that his former hesitations arose from perfectionism, not ignorance, and sensed a kind of shyness and confusion, which we found endearing but irritating when examinations loomed (not that we aliens understood much of Irish history).

Many would-be mimics tried to remember his glorious mispronunciations, gigantic sentences and abuse of parentheses within parentheses – all that I can remember is the magic phrase (abandoning his papers and coming forward, almost secretively), 'Youneedn'tputthisinyournotes,' introducing some precious comments of enormous value, coming as they did from his historical judgment, which on a fellow-specialist's page would have been supported by endless footnotes. JOSEPH GOY (1953)

In my time at TCD, they said that he would start a lecture to be held in the Museum building at the GMB on his way there. Five minutes of the lecture was thus lost on the birds in Front Square. He tended to wear a lot of clothing, even in summer – scarf and heavy coat, plus several sweaters. RONALD N.G. FERGUSON (1972)

A story about Professor McDowell's punctuality: he started and ended his lectures very much on time and once it was noted by an undergraduate that the Professor, on a bus coming down Dawson Street, which had been delayed by an accident in Rathmines, at 10 o'clock precisely, began to talk in a hurried voice, very clearly, about

Machiavelli and Florence. Much to the amusement of all those on the lower deck of the bus, he continued to talk and gesticulate, even while getting off the bus in Suffolk Street. The undergraduate, who shall be nameless, followed the Professor down to the Front Gate (he was still talking about Machiavelli and the Prince) and, keeping a discreet distance from him, across Front Square, where many people stopped and looked and smiled at the Professor, talking excitedly; he saw Professor McDowell enter his lecture room and close the door. To his own satisfaction and to the amusement of many others, he had begun his lecture on time – even though it was on a bus and his audience was not composed of undergraduates!

NORMAN H. LUSH (1951)

He lectures with total irrelevance and on a heroic scale of either boredom or amusement, depending on taste, on sixteenth-century military history and on the foibles of the characters and personalities in this period. Robert Brendan McDowell is perhaps guilty of excessive self-indulgence, in lecturing on what interests him, rather than on what students might find informative. But many would not miss his lectures for the world, despite his inevitably late arrival and his tendency to forget his notes. TRINITY NEWS 23.2.1961

Anyone fortunate enough to have been one of his students can vouch for the fact that Doctor McDowell's lectures were quite unique. In fact, I think that he has to have been the only Don who could lecture on two quite independent subjects at one and the same time. For an aperitif we would have the roll-call, a ritual which held little interest for him, since he had long given up trying to work out how five people present could have forty other personalities. Thus, the roll was never really called – it was more of an overture for the main event – or a shoe-horn for seguing into the lecture.

'Armitage?' he would call. 'Armitage Allen Miss Allen Ainsworth Arthur Azu-azzoo--azzoob-some sort of I don't know I would imagine I would *imagine some* sort of foreign-sounding name well it certainly isn't an Irish name Baddely Bradshaw Babington which is I fink where we left orf last week wif er wif er ve wif Babington and his erm

RB McDowell as a house guest in Belgium, *c.* 1984.

PHOTO: ROB VAN MESDAG

his erm – his ah *plot*. Is Babington here by the way?'

At which point five voices would answer in the affirmative.

TERENCE BRADY (1961)

I read History and took Anglicanism in the eighteenth century as a special subject with Dr McDowell in 1964–65. He adopted a rather relaxed approach to the subject and delighted in telling anecdotes about various clergymen and other figures. He didn't pursue the Term Essay and, in Finals, set some curious questions. I recall that he was very helpful and well-disposed towards students. He showed deep concern for the College as an institution, with love of its past, some regrets for the changes and concern for its future.

PETER IRONS (1966)

I was at Trinity from 1962 to 1966 and studied Modern History and Political Science, so I saw quite a lot of him. He was responsible for giving us lectures in our second year on European History, covering the broad span of *circa* 1500 to 1815. Deviations galore! – especially on some of the more exotic aspects of Voltaire's life and those of other artists – and then the last minute realization that he had still to give a coherent lecture on eighteenth-century France. For that particular lecture, having warned us that he would be talking very fast, without deviation or hesitation, although possibly some repetition, he mach-ine-gunned his way through the required syllabus.

ROGER KYNASTON (1966)

My first memories of Professor RB McDowell are of his lectures on medieval Irish history in the large Regent House room, where the acoustics were poor and the subject dauntingly obscure, to a new arrival from England like myself. He adopted a happy-go-lucky atti-tude to certain dates of, 'Give or take a couple of hundred years,' which somehow added to my confusion. However, his lectures were appreciated. There was an occasion when our assembly of Junior Fresh waiting expectantly in this upper room had evidently slipped through academic consciousness, but one of our number spied Dr McDowell wandering through Front Square and ran down to ambush him and inform him that he should be attending to us. Very amiably, he agreed to this proposition (the fact that the Junior Fresher was a remarkably glamorous girl had, of course, nothing to do with it) and so we were treated to an extra discourse, while the Senior Sophisters, whose turn it really was, languished neglected.

Later, some of us submitted essays on eighteenth-century English History to him and he was liberal in his reception of our meagre efforts. As we sat in his rooms reading our corrected writings, he enlivened the proceedings by throwing balls of crumpled paper over our heads, in the general direction of a distant waste-paper basket.
JENNIFER MILLER (HART) (1954)

We always enjoyed his lectures (he was known to us as 'McD') and seeing his long scarf and hat, which never changed during the four years. We still recall the odd socks and his nearly putting one of us out of the Classics Library for talking.
KATE SHELMERDINE (1950)

Dr McDowell was tutor to me and to my room-mate in Botany Bay. Tutors then were more concerned with social than academic matters and we were delighted to tempt him round one evening, by having available a good bottle of sherry. COLIN TITE (1956)

A remarkable man who was greatly loved by his students.
ELEANOR BURMAN (1952)

He once came in during a rare snowy winter, to lecture on something of an Irish nature, but, attracted by the sight of Front Square all white, proceeded to talk for an hour on the Bolshevik Revolution and his views on it. DR JILL SHEPPARD (ROBBINS) (1957)

I have always been amused at myself for objecting to people reading for a first degree being termed 'students', because I heard McDowell explain, in my 'formative years', that 'undergraduate' was correct. How right of him to hold on to academic punctilio amid changing times. DR KATHLEEN WELLS (MacLARNON) (1950)

Most students will have had the task of presenting a piece of written work on a particular subject to a lecturer during their time in College. Many will have presented their work to Dr McDowell. Some of that number may have had my experience of doing this over breakfast. I arrived at the appointed hour, 9 a.m.: 'Doughty, come in, come in. Do sit down.' He then produced a large cake-tin and removed a large fruitcake and proceeded to cut a very substantial piece and pour out a glass of milk. 'Would you prefer it if I returned later, Professor McDowell?' I said, 'No, no, no,' he replied and so he proceeded to critically study my work and then enquired how preparations were going for Trinity Regatta.

SIR WILLIAM DOUGHTY (1953)

Memorable Journeys

FLORENCE

He went on holiday to Italy in one long vacation (1948) in a motorbike and sidecar, with a contemporary of mine, Nigel Pratt – RB riding in the sidecar. They had a row or just lost each other somewhere on the way across France and then met up again, by chance, on the banks of the Arno, in Florence. HENRY CLARK (1950)

ROME

My brother-in-law, Nigel Pratt, went on holiday with him to Italy when he was an undergraduate (Nigel, that is). It seems that at Rome Station, when they were planning to go south to Naples, Nigel placed the unsuspecting McDowell on a train to Venice.

Happily, their relationship recovered, after Nigel returned from Naples and McDowell supposedly from Venice. They are still close friends! LORD HASKINS (CHRIS HASKINS) (1959)

MILAN

A story which went the rounds of TCD – then, of course, a much smaller community than now – when we got back, concerned a trip which we made together in the summer of 1948 or 1949. Brendan proposed that we should visit Italy and I (who of course hadn't been there before, or perhaps only once before), enthusiastically agreed.

We duly set off and arrived at Milan railway station to board the train to Florence.

The train drew into the platform and I promptly boarded it. But McD didn't (I don't know why – perhaps I wasn't a good enough Cicerone). Anyway, I duly arrived in Florence that evening without him and put up in some *pensione*. The following morning, I went on to the Lungoarno and was amazed to find him at my elbow – I still don't know how he managed it. NIGEL PRATT (1950)

DR McDOWELL EXPLAINS:

What in fact happened was that, owing to a muddle, we were separated on the platform at Lausanne, took separate trains, but made for what we had previously agreed was going to be our next stop and after forty-eight hours were reunited on the banks of the Arno in Florence.

THE JOURNEY CONTINUES:

Then our adventures took a fresh turn, because the leader of the Italian Communist party, one Palmiro Togliatti, was assassinated. The streets consequently were filled with *carabinieri* in jeeps, fully armed. My inclination was to seek the shelter of the *pensione* forthwith, but McD astounded me by declaring that this was an historic happening which he, as an historian, was bound to witness. So, I had to accompany him round the streets, in imminent expectation of being shot (which, luckily, didn't happen).

But McD didn't turn a hair! In the days following, we did the usual tourist round of the Palazzo Vecchio, the Uffizi, the gardens, etc. After that, we parted, this time by design, though again I can't quite remember why, except perhaps that he may have had something else to do, which I hadn't.

So, I went alone by train to Venice, which, to an undergraduate, was a marvellous experience – the arrival at the station (which is at the far end of the Grand Canal), the journey up by *vaporetto* and by Rialto to St Mark's Square, where an orchestra was playing suitable music *en plein air* in the Italian night. I thought that I had died and gone to heaven!

Ehen fugaces – I expect that as an alumnus of TCD you have Latin. I found myself, during our many peregrinations, translating inscriptions, so I may have been useful in that way and we did undertake other journeys in Ireland, Britain and France (and maybe elsewhere).
NIGEL PRATT (1950)

PERUGIA – ROME – NAPLES

Indeed I did go on holiday with McDowell – in 1952. He usually went on holiday with one of the Pratt brothers who was, as I remember, a judge somewhere in the British Colonial Service. Anyway, he couldn't go at the last minute, so RB asked me if I would spend ten days or so travelling through Italy with him. Now to the point: as JD, he was in charge of the Library, so he borrowed an 1880 edition of Baedecker, to guide us on our way. In Perugia, en route to Rome, we were advised to 'hire a platoon of carabinieri to protect us from brigands'. What those same brigands would have thought of McD beggars belief. However, eventually we arrived in Rome and toured the various galleries and ate very little – pasta once per day – as we were both impoverished. We intended to stay with the Tomacellis on Ischia – a somewhat loose arrangement.

Now for the nub: We arrived at Naples station, still to be repaired. It was high summer and McDowell was clad in his renowned navy-blue muffler and his battered pork-pie hat. I left him to guard the cases just outside the main entrance and went off to find lodgings for the night. When I returned he was surrounded by a group of boys anxious to carry our bags. The tallest and strongest, not surprisingly, got the job and we headed off to a café near the city centre. When we arrived it was McDowell's turn to tip and he offered the boy a ten-lira note (worth approximately one old penny). The boy shouted in disbelief and took a step back into the road, causing three cars to bump each other – there was mayhem, with the boy running off still shouting imprecations at McDowell, but not wishing to remain at the scene. McDowell turned to me and said, 'I must say he seemed to be very pleased with his tip. Did I give him too much?'
ALAN COOK (1955)

GREECE

DR McDOWELL

*J*eremy Lewes [Lewis], *biographer of Cyril Connolly, in his autobiography relates meeting me at Delphi and that I, 'a lonely determined figure, strode off to walk to Athens'.*

*In fact, I had a very pleasant meeting c. 1962 with Lewes and
some friends of his in an out-of-the-way corner of Venice. They were
on their way to Greece via the Adriatic. I had just come up that sea
from Greece. I talked of my travels and almost certainly mentioned
Delphi. Incidentally, during all this marvellous holiday – a great
sweep from Vienna to Venice, through the Balkans – I had a most
congenial companion, but on the day I met Lewes, having had an
enjoyable lunch, we were surveying Venice independently, before
meeting for dinner.*

I remember in Greece on the island of Euboia, I had an old naval
friend staying, full Admiral and, as it happened, Second Sea Lord. He
said to RB, 'For God's sake, McDowell, if you will leave your clothes
outside your door, I will wash them!' Nothing came of it.

There was always a mystery about where McDowell liked to swim,
which he claimed he liked to do from an isolated beach, half a mile
from the house. I remember an occasion when we were all at lunch
on the terrace, which looked down on a lower coast road. Suddenly
there appeared, walking alone along the road coming home to lunch,
a figure without any trousers – McDowell in tweed upper part of his
suit, squashed pork-pie hat and scarf. On arrival, he enthused 'It was
lovely and cool!' ANTHONY MARECCO

I always think of something I read a long time ago in a travel book
written by Douglas Kennedy, who was at TCD after us. So far as I
remember, DK was exploring some ruins in a remote part of Greece,
when he saw a familiar figure wearing hat, coat and scarf coming
down the road, who turned out to be the JD. So maybe he is ubiqui-
tous as well as everlasting. JOANNA BONAR-LAW (1961)

NORWAY

In about 1971 RB bravely visited my mother's Norwegian property, consisting of wooden huts in a forest by a fjord. He was known to abhor the cold and he wrapped up for the occasion. However, he also rowed a boat and swam in the glacier-melted fjord, in a pair of black shorts, and then picnicked with us on a glacier in the snowy Jotunheim mountains, showing that he could endure the worst conditions with a smile and a stream of commentary.
PATRICK GUINNESS (1980)

GENEVA

I remember him being a good chum of Richard Stack, all beard and Gauloise smoke. Stack, who lived in Geneva, and the JD once went on a European trip in an old Buick, I think – an incongruous sight they must have been! DAVID GILLIAT (1961)

MOSCOW

Anyone who follows Dr McD into a bathroom may observe that the wash basin plug has been removed from the sink and is hanging over the edge by its chain. There is a reason for this. According to Dr McD, when he was staying in a hotel in Moscow or Leningrad, when it was still the Soviet Union, he came back to his room one day, only to find a lot of fuss and carrying-on outside his door, water seeping under the door and himself being clearly, if incomprehensibly (because it was in Russian), berated by the floor *dezhurnaya* (the sort of concierge/floor matron person you did and possibly still do get in Russian hotels). When they got in, they found that he had left the plug in the wash basin and the water was still flowing. He told us that he thought that they were going to haul him off to the Lefortovo (or whichever prison would be the appropriate one) and that he would end his days in the Gulag, for the crime of damaging State property. And thus, since then, he has made it a habit to toss the plug out of the sink and out of danger … I must say that the thought of him being x-q'd by the KGB and what this would do for the morale of the KGB, was quite …inspirational… HEATHER O'BRIEN (LASKY) (1961)

THE KING'S ROAD

'THE NAME'S McDOWELL'

One evening in 2001, when the 22 bus on Putney Common drove off without RB, he and I chased it along the New King's Road by car. RB commented that it was as though we were in a James Bond film – such excitement – 007 McDowell and Moneypenny Lyons! JENNIFER LYONS (MRS F.S.L. LYONS)

'NO NOT JEMEPPE…WE WANT GENAPPE'
Rob van Mesdag entertained Dr McDowell in Belgium

ARRIVAL

Friends in London had encouraged RB to renew his knowledge of Belgium, by visiting me in Brussels, where I lived in the 1980s. He loved the idea and disembarked at the city's south station. I had warned him, 'As the place is like a warren – corridors and exits everywhere – let's meet at the "International Ticket Office", because there is only one of those. Please ask people to direct you to it.'

Did he? All I remember – after a long wait – is a hat, overcoat and umbrella of unmistakable identity walking backwards and bumping into me. I stopped it and welcomed my guest to Brussels. But my greeting was not acknowledged. Instead, RB pointed to an exit, saying: 'They are all alike, there are no signs and they don't correspond. I kept going round and round.' I knew he would.

Waterloo rated high in the places that RB was interested in visiting and no sooner did we approach the town, than he took the lead, suggesting: 'We might start by taking a look at Lord Uxbridge's wooden leg; then go to the Wellington Museum and thereafter visit the Waterloo panorama.' This we did and as we found ourselves at the foot of the Butte du Lion, the mini pyramid with its lion on top, we climbed it, for a panoramic view of the battlefield. Reaching the viewing platform after a climb of two hundred steps, RB noted with some self-satisfaction: 'Not bad for someone well into his seventies.'

Next, it was suggested that we drive to monuments such as the one commemorating Sir Alexander Gordon, one of Wellington's officers, and to one in honour of the Prussians, Belgians, French and others who were killed and we visited locations such as Quatres Bras, Hougoumont, Plancenoit and Belle Alliance. After visiting the farm, Le Caillou, Napoleon's headquarters, RB suggested that we motor to Genappe to look for a monument or plaque commemorating France's last rearguard action at that place.

Becoming a little confused after so many names of places visited, in French and Flemish, I was relieved to see a signpost indicating 'Jemeppe', and assumed it to be the Flemish equivalent of the Genappe in Walloon. So, I checked with RB: 'Is this what we are looking for?' His response was immediate, as if he had been there the day before: 'No not Jemeppe … we want Genappe.'

MADAME BISSCHOT

That night, in the hallway of the apartment of Madame Bisschot, my landlady, who lived on the floor below me, plans were made for the next day. She had kindly offered RB her spare bedroom and while we were talking she noticed that RB had his hand on the door handle of what he thought was his room. But it wasn't. It was the broom cupboard next to it. She gave me an anxious look as if to say, 'If he's not careful …'

A discussion took place about wake-up time and breakfast the next morning. 'At what time would Monsieur like a call and does he have café, fromage, confiture, petit pain, fruits …?' After some five minutes or so, all had been arranged and Madame, her gaze still fixed firmly on the door handle, wished us goodnight. But she remained where she stood, looking at me maliciously. 'This could be fun,' she must have thought. It was. RB opened the door assuredly and stepped resolutely into the cupboard. There was much laughter in the hallway that night, not least from RB himself.

ACID TEST

We visited some of the First World War cemeteries near Ypres and the town itself and its Mennin Gate. Later, I took RB to see the nine-teenth-century hydraulic barge lifts on the Canal du Centre and back in Brussels I showed him my rowing club, where he took great interest in my new sculls, made of carbon instead of wood. On another day, Antwerp was on our programme. It was to be the location of a test of his memory of the names of two Trinity graduates: Gilles Thal Larsen and his wife Anne, *née* Slattery, who live in southern Holland, one hour away from Antwerp. Gilles and I had concocted the following plan. RB and I were to have a drink on the terrace of one of the cafés in the Market and he and Anne were to walk past, pretending to look for a place for themselves.

Our trick worked beautifully: 'Well, if it isn't Dr McDowell … how nice to see you here in Antwerp, what brings you to this place?' Gilles and Anne exclaimed as they found us. While getting up to shake hands, RB needed only one second before reciprocating their delight with: 'Oh yes, of course, Thal Larsen.' Having passed this acid test, the Thal Larsens and I treated RB to dinner in a nearby fish restaurant. Gilles, alas, died in 2001.

GOODBYE

RB's departure took the usual shape:

'Now I thhhhink I should allow myself plenty of time … you see what I mean … I mean trains in Belgium I expecttt are, shall I say, ehh will be running on time … it's not as if we are in … well, let's say Liverpool … I have packed my bag very comfortably and am all ready … so I don't think I will want a coffee, no thank you … let me find my watch … it's now a good half hour before … do you also make it ten o'clock … can you drive right up to the station … you know what I mean eh, eh, some stations can no longer be reached unless one takes a taxi … so if you don't minnnnd … ehh it's been very pleasant … you know what I mean … I don't suppose you know which platform my train leaves from … I expect there will be signs … I mean there must be several trains a day to Calais … or will the signs say "London"… now if you don't mind … where's your car … now I thhhhink…'
ROB VAN MESDAG (1951)

'McDowell laughing'
PHOTO: BRYAN MCGOVERN

Myths and Legends

Dr McDowell's role as JD took on a mythical status and what people did not know about him, they made up. There were a number of favourite tales that went the rounds of TCD for years, in multiple and often contradictory versions and, after forty years or so, who is to say which account is true? For this reason, varying versions are given below, so that readers can choose their own favourite. A.L.

From what I remember of those high days of Trinity storytelling, the truth was not allowed to get in the way of a good yarn!
LT.-COL. ROBIN ANDERSON (1961)

DR McDOWELL COMMENTS:

I think Robin Anderson is very sound about Trinity story-telling when he says, 'Truth was not allowed to get in the way!' This is a rare opportunity for a person who is a legend to be able to correct some of the stories, on the assumption my memory is not bad. People are very unreliable when it comes to repeating a story! There is a curious way in which people don't test very carefully what they are saying, when striving after effect. I am very interested in accuracy and believe how unreliable is the human memory, or, at least, how it has to be tested very hard.

'All memories are false,' said Salman Rushdie, and who am I to quibble with so great an author? DR JIM O'BRIEN (1961)

[117]

THE GUN IN FRONT SQUARE
Six accounts of this famous tale:

O N E : An incident in the Trinity term. It was known that, after Commons, RB walked down the steps of the Dining Hall, under the Campanile and back to his rooms. On a particular evening, two undergraduate men walked ahead of him between the Campanile and the Rubrics, on either side of the gravel. Half-way down, a shot rang out and the chap on the left fell down, clutching his head; after two seconds there was another shot and the man on the right collapsed, grasping his chest – then a very loud voice boomed out, 'McDowell – you're next!' whereupon the terrified RB turned around and, holding his hat and scarf, rapidly made for the Porters' Lodge at the Front Gate.
This was a contrived incident and there were no serious repercussions, but to those witnessing the sight of RB sprinting across Front Square, shouting, 'Murder! Murder!' it was quite a scene.
NORMAN LUSH (1951) & NICOLA LUSH-MCCRUM (1982)

T W O : This definitely happened during my second year at Trinity in 1965. I was living in Front Square at the time. A group of students decided to lure RB McD into a trap one evening, just as they were about to lock the main entrance, at midnight. RB McD had a habit of returning through Front Gate around that time, probably to catch students who were being rowdy or trying to smuggle totty in with them. Anyway, one of my contemporaries, whose name I forget, (from Northern Ireland, I think) was rolling down Grafton Street very much the worse for alcohol, with RB McD following him at a distance. Having got through the Front Gate the drunken student was staggering towards the Campanile, just as RB McD, in hot pursuit, was emerging into Front Square. At that moment, a gun was fired from one of the third Floor Front Square windows and the student immediately fell to the ground, dead. In the silence that followed, a voice boomed, 'You're next, McDowell,' whereupon RB McD turned and fled back to the cover of Front Gate and the dead student scarpered. After all these years, the identity of the perpetrator is still unknown.
GEOFFREY KELLY (1967)

THREE: The story goes that McDowell, who was Junior Dean at the time, had annoyed a residential student over some issue or another and there was bad blood between them (he may even have had him sent down). This student knew McDowell's habits and that he left the Dining Hall at a certain time and headed for the (old) Library. He schooled a few of his friends to be casually walking with McDowell – or towards him – at that time. He then set himself up in his rooms with a rifle and a series of blanks. When McDowell came out of the Dining Hall, the student fired and one of his friends fell to the ground. Another shot and another victim. After three or four had fallen and the JD was much perplexed, the student shouted, 'Right, McDowell, You're next!' Whereupon the Junior Dean gathered his robes about him and fled for the Library. All the 'victims' then promptly got up and walked away, leaving no evidence of the crime.
JOHN WILSON (1971)

FOUR: A Junior Dean doing his night rounds in the eighteenth century had been shot, the story goes. Two centuries on, RB McDowell was doing his night rounds as Junior Dean, when a shot rang out as he approached Botany Bay and a man walking nearby fell to the ground clutching, his chest. 'You're next, McDowell!' a voice called out from a darkened window above him. The culprits were caught and, I think, severely punished. PATRICIA REIDY (1964)

FIVE: McDowell was walking across Front Square. A student was walking beside him. There was a loud crack. The student fell to the ground with a blood-coloured liquid oozing from his chest. A voice called out over the square, 'The next one's for you, McDowell.'
CANON PETER NORTON (1961)

SIX: Denis Trimingham (West London area, in 1964) and Billy Mc-Loughlin (Northern Ireland) had some kind of explosive noise resembling gunfire handy in Front Square, one evening. As the JD started out across the Square from his rooms, Billy appeared to shoot Denis (or vice versa) from across the Square. Denis fell 'dead' in good view

of the JD, whereupon Billy shouted to the JD, 'You're next, McDowell!' and turned towards him. The JD fell flat on the ground to save
his life. I forget what happened next!
TIM WILLCOCKS (1964)

Regarding the name of the Northern Irish student who might know
more about the shooting scam, Robin Verso said that there was a guy
during our time at Trinity called 'Nelson' and that seems to ring a bell
with me. Maybe that little clue will give you a lead!
GEOFFREY KELLY (1967)

DR MCDOWELL COMMENTS:

*N*ever *happened! In the Front Square, an undergraduate points a
gun (shotgun) at me. I panic and either run away or fall on the
ground, shrieking! I would have remembered, because from a very
early age, I was strictly told never to point a gun at anyone (especially if I was aware that it was loaded) and, also, I was taught that a gun
must always be carried with the muzzle pointed to the ground. It was
George Wilkins, in his few unhappy days as JD in 1885, who was followed, it is said, by undergraduates who were pointing guns at him,
and who only lasted as JD for three or four days. He was most unsuit-
able for the job. I heard the story and more than once repeated it.*

PAGANS
Five versions:

ONE: THE MOON WORSHIPPER
At some time around the 1950s, a student, residing in Trinity College,
Dublin, was asked by the Junior Dean to explain his failure to attend
College Chapel, to fulfil his obligations under the rules of the College.
The student told the Junior Dean that the reason for his non-atten-
dance at Chapel was due to the fact that he was a Moon Worshipper.
The JD said that he had made a note of this reply. Some weeks later,
towards midnight on a cold night during the same term, the student
was disturbed by a knock on the door of his rooms and, upon opening it, he found the Junior Dean confronting him. The student said

that he was very surprised to see the JD at such a late hour, where-upon the JD told him that, as there was a full moon that night, he had called to take the student to College Park, where he could fulfil the obligations of his stated religion, by the light of the celestial object. It is not known whether the student appeared at College Chapel the following Sunday.   FELICITY McNAB (MELDRUM)(1953)

TWO: THE SUN WORSHIPPER
In the days when McDowell was Junior Dean, students had to declare their religion when they entered College and were only able to change their religion at the end of term. In those days, students were expected to attend their church on Sundays. One smart student declared himself as a Sun Worshipper. On his first Saturday night, he duly retired, slightly inebriated, comfortable in the thought of a late rising on the Sunday morning. At about 4 a.m. there was a loud knocking at his door. He scrambled out of bed and opened the door to find McDowell, who stated that, as Junior Dean, it was his duty to ensure that the students conformed to their religions and he expected this Sun Worshipper to be up at dawn every Sunday, to greet the Sun God as it rose into the sky.   SAM DARBY (1975)

THREE: At the time when the incident occurred, there was a College regulation which required all students in residence to notify the Junior Dean of their religious denomination and to attend the service appropriate to their faith, at least once a week. One individual, seeking to circumvent this regulation, declared his religion as 'Sun Worshipper'. A few days later, a skip knocked on his door at an early hour, with the greeting, 'Good morning, Sir. The Junior Dean sends his compliments and asks me to inform you that the time is 5 a.m. and the sun is just about to rise!' MICHAEL POWELL (1971)

FOUR: Stories that I heard: There's a requirement for all applicants to put their religion on their forms, in the sixties. Someone put 'Sun Worshipper' and, for the first term in his freshman year, McDowell was around to rooms to get him up at dawn!
PATRICK O'SULLIVAN (1971)

FIVE: In the era of compulsory Chapel attendance, two residents sought exemption, on the grounds that they were Sun Worshippers. Shortly after 4 a.m. one Sunday, they were awakened by loud knocking on their room door. A College porter addressed the bleary-eyed residents, 'Dr McDowell presents his compliments. Sun worship begins in College Park in ten minutes.'

When I asked RB about this story, he dismissed it, 'That story is told about every Junior Dean in every college I have visited.'

The well-loved RB shares with Mahaffy, the subject of one of his biographies, the characteristic that stories become attached to him.
DR SEAN BARRETT (JUNIOR DEAN 1986–2000)

THE READING ROOM, THE LIBRARY AND THE LADDER

O*ne of the first tales that a Junior Freshman would hear, on arriving in College, was that Dr McDowell had fallen off a ladder. The tenacious hold of this dubious tale on the collective psyche is a mystery. As stories go, it is a non-event – nobody saw it happen; nobody knows whether it was in the Reading Room or in the Library; whether the Professor was injured or not and not even* Trinity News *has any record of the event.* A.L.

Nevertheless, here are eight sample versions:

ONE: That incident in the *Reading Room* – everyone probably knows it! He was up on a ladder in the gallery, looking at a reference. When finished, he put the book back on the shelf, forgot that he was on a ladder and walked straight off, *breaking a collarbone and some other attachment.* REV. CLIFFORD COMYNS (1950)

TWO: Another time, he climbed the *library steps* and stayed on the top so long, reading a book, that *he stepped off* and fell on the floor. *He got up and walked away.* ELEANOR BURMAN (1952)

THREE: Professor McDowell *was sitting* on a ladder in the *Reading Room*, perusing a book from the shelves. When he had finished, he replaced the book and stepped away, forgetting where he had been sitting. KATE TIMMS (1952)

FOUR: The JD was up a library ladder in the *Reading Room*, in 1958 or so, and, after a long search on a top shelf, he found the book that he wanted. Excited at the find, he opened the book and stepped back to read it, falling several feet to the floor and *breaking his leg*. CANON PETER NORTON (1961)

FIVE: My wife (Anne Jones that was) tells how Dr McDowell was on top of a stepladder in the *Reading Room* of the Trinity Library, deeply engaged in a book, one day in the late 1950s, when he walked off and crashed, *unharmed*, to the floor. GERRY BLANCHARD (1965)

SIX: I remember that he was on the high steps in the *Long Room* and simply walked off, without realizing that there was a drop, such was his total immersion in the subject at hand. STEPHEN RICHARDSON (1972)

SEVEN: Professor McDowell was rumoured to have been in the *Old Library* and climbed one of the rolling ladders, read a book, forgot where he was, turned around, went to walk away and so fell off the ladder. SAM DARBY (1975)

EIGHT: I suppose that everyone knows the apocryphal one about him being engrossed, reading, at the top of the ladder in the *Old Library*, when he spied another interesting book a couple of shelves to his left. Completely forgetting where he was, he apparently crashed to the ground, stepping out to reach it. GEOFFREY KELLY (1967)

Tally: *3 x Old Library; 5 x Reading Room; 2 x injured; 3 not injured.*

POSSIBLE EXPLANATION:
He regularly entertained those of us 'in College' in the 1956 to 1959 period, who used the Reading Room at night to keep warm, dropping

books and occasionally forgetting that he was standing on a ladder. No, I never saw him fall off, but it was alleged to have happened and many of us scientists, 'in from the cold' used to watch and wait for it to happen. I think that it was probably fabricated by Law and History students, to impress on those not in the Reading Room during the day what they had missed! DR I.K. FERGUSON OBE (1964)

DR MCDOWELL COMMENTS:

I *don't think I ever fell, but Professor Moody did. Professor Moody had a nasty fall and it was attributed to me. I continued, until quite a late age, to go up ladders.*

I did decide when I was seventy not to go up ladders in the Gallery – you looked down 60 to 70 feet! [See front cover, A.L.]

THE TRAIN TO BELFAST

A *nother myth was the one about the Junior Freshman who sets off for Belfast by train, at the end of his first term. He falls into conversation with a charming lady, who listens attentively to his excited tales of life at Trinity and of the amazing Junior Dean. As the train draws into Belfast, the lady pauses at the door, smiles and says, 'And, to think – my other son is perfectly normal!'*

No matter that Dr McDowell didn't have a brother – this tale went the rounds for years. A.L.

THREE MORE VERSIONS OF THIS OLD CHESTNUT:
No story about the JD is complete without an anecdote and my favourite one remains the story recounted about the train journey. A student was travelling back *from Belfast* by train and was busy studying for his examinations. A woman sitting next to him asked him if he was at TCD. Replying in the affirmative, she then asked him if he knew McDowell. He said, 'yes' and started to laugh. She joined in and they sat there, laughing together. The woman then stopped laughing for a moment and said, 'It's lucky my other son is more normal.' True or false, it's a nice story.
TRINITY NEWS 1.2.1962

TCD student regales lady in train *going to Dublin* with idiosyncrasies of Dr McD. When train stops at Amiens Street Station, lady says, 'Well, my other son is normal!' JOY WHITE (1960)

An undergraduate was *returning to his digs*, after lectures. *On the bus*, he sat by a lady who said to him, 'I see by your scarf that you attend Trinity College. Do you know the Junior Dean?' 'Heavens, yes,' replied the student. 'He's a most odd character, wanders around Front Square wearing a long scarf and talks to himself all the time. I think that he must be slightly mad!' The lady rose to leave the bus and said, 'I have other children who are quite normal!'
DR THOMAS ROSS (1963)

NO TRUTH IN THE RUMOUR...

The time has come to declare that:
- he never read out his laundry list in lieu of the next page of his lecture notes
- he never came into the Reading Room wearing his pyjamas under his overcoat
- he never repeated the same lecture three times
- he was never found drunk and incapable in the Provost's Garden, etc.

These are merely tales resulting from some tiny true detail which, in a community hungry for gossip and obsessed with social reputations, became successively exaggerated, but always in a spirit of affection, as for one's favourite uncle.
JOSEPH GOY (1953)

There was a myth current in my day that his skip once made his bed without realizing that he was still in it. H.R.F. KEATING (1952)

DR McDOWELL COMMENTS
on yet another tall story:
In his autobiography, William Trevor refers to me as, 'scurrying past prostitutes on my first visit to London'.

I paid my first visit to London at the age of eleven! I went there frequently meeting relations. From the end of the war, for some years, soliciting spread widely through the West End. Naturally, I (and others) got to know well by sight a number of the 'solicitors' (good-looking girls) and the problem that I heard discussed was, how to combine an acknowledgment of having seen one another before, with a polite rejection of their services. Almost certainly I talked about this in Trinity to Trevor, whom I don't recollect meeting much socially, but who knew people I knew. It's a garbled account of what I said.

Friendship

We always called him McDowell; he stuck to the pre-war custom among men, and particularly academics, of using the unadorned surname. The tide of Christian naming proved too strong after a bit for my wife Sue, who, at a certain point, began calling him Brendan; she must have done some sleuthing. He was a friend of mine from the 1950s, that is, for a great part of my life. In his hat, muffler and grey jersey, he was a sort of anti-icon and all the better for that. Wonderful company, the source and subject of endless stories.

LORD MOYNE (THE HON. JONATHAN GUINNESS)

McDowell and I had a close common friend in the late Alexander Lieven, an undergraduate a year junior to myself. McDowell, who loved titles, in an innocent sort of way – which reminded me of Proust – was very excited about Lieven's arrival, which he announced to me, as follows: 'He's a Russian Prince! A real Russian Prince! I looked him up in Gotha.' And so he was. McDowell later shared rooms in College with Lieven and they were the most untidy set of rooms that can ever have been shared by a prince and a commoner.

DR CONOR CRUISE O'BRIEN (1940)

RB has many remarkable qualities. He has made, and keeps, hundreds of close friends of many different sorts and he is very amusing

company, with an amazing memory. He can talk well, and rather fast, on almost any topic which crops up. He takes a shrewd and amusing view of quite small social nuances. He's also, at his best, one of the better after-dinner speakers I've ever heard. He is still, to this day, very hard-working with his historical research. Oddly, he is not a good correspondent or letter-writer and seldom, if ever, sends Christmas cards. He is a very special person who may yet outlive his older friends, but he is not someone who should ever be forgotten.
HENRY CLARK (1950)

I was never a close friend, although, all my life, whenever we met, he had the generous ability to make me feel that I was the one person that he longed to meet. DR RICHARD MCCLELLAND (1943)

In 1953 there was a reigning college beauty, a blonde, who was always accompanied by her dark-haired friend. I can't remember their names, but he certainly accompanied one or the other – or was it both? – to some College parties, that year.
DR JILL SHEPPARD (ROBBINS) 1957

RB's special girlfriends in the years 1947 to 1953, which he has described as vintage Trinity years, were an unlikely couple – Joan Schellenburg, from a Yorkshire county family and Iris Quinn, a rather beautiful and very well-dressed, fair-haired girl from Portadown (you knew it as soon as she opened her mouth), whose father, it was said, had won a big prize in the Irish Sweep. They would take RB, or he would take them, to College dances in the Metropole, where he never did much dancing, but he chatted to everyone. He always referred to them just as 'Joan and Iris'. Sadly, Joan died quite young and I don't know what happened to Iris. HENRY CLARK (1950)

MEMORIES OF A LONG FRIENDSHIP

In College days, meeting in the Front Square of an evening, coming up to rooms for coffee, he suggests a walk through small gate into Nassau Street. Has bunch of keys.

Going for a walk, often in back streets, explaining the glories of Regency Dublin. This was usually in the early hours of the morning.

Coming back from Islandbridge (Boat Club) after a party. I was sitting on the roof-rack of Hugh Delap's model-Y Ford, with a girl-friend. RB, inside, insists that he must offer his seat to a lady.

The cheering of RB coming into Commons after coxing staff to victory at Trinity Regatta (as a victorious cox he had been immersed in water by his crew!).

More recently, my dog Boris pinching his hat, at a party at my house.

After my Commencement, at a dance at the Shelbourne Rooms. They wanted to throw me out and he would not let them.

Other things are going for walks with him on Sundays, sometimes outside Dublin, occasionally to Dublin Zoo.
JOHN PEARSON (1956)

His friendship with David Webb – it appeared very much the Mutt and Jeff of the *Evening Herald* cartoon-strip. Another claimant to that comparison was Paul Keating, later Ambassador and father of Geoffrey and George Jeffrey (former cricketer, scholar and car salesman!). ERIC EARLE (1947)

I had left Trinity before the *History of Medieval Ireland*, written by another of our lecturers, Professor Jocelyn Otway-Ruthven, was published, in 1968. She was a lady of formidable appearance and manner, who was also actually very good to students and who took the trouble to entertain us in her house. Tragically, for a scholar of such distinction, she was incapacitated by a bad stroke for years before her death and Professor McDowell was very kind in visiting her. She could not speak and, though he was extremely talkative by nature, even he found it difficult to carry on a conversation when there was no response. JENNIFER MILLER (HART) (1954)

I was in Trinity from 1948 to 1952 and in fact did not go back until

last year, on the fiftieth anniversary of my graduation, for the Annual Reunion. After fifty years, I still have happy memories of Roddy
McDowell, going up and down the Front Square, with a scarf casually around his neck. He was always pleasant and helpful to foreign
students like myself and his high-pitched voice when he was a speaker at Society meetings and his sense of humour are memories that I
will always carry.
MAHOMED J. JAFFER (1952)

RB has been a good friend to me for very many years and I value this
friendship and his advice on literary matters, greatly. I remember driving across London, early on the morning of his 80th birthday, to
deliver his new grey pullover, before he set out for the Institute and
singing, 'Happy Birthday', at the top of my voice outside his hall door,
only to be informed by two startled, dungareed, painters upstairs, that
he was in Ireland and was not expected to return for a week.
JENNIFER LYONS (MRS F.S.L. LYONS)

He was very, very kind. He was kind to everyone. He was very kind
to me. I can't think why. JILL MCEVEDY (1961)

Despite being much younger than RB (I'm forty-six), I can't think of
many of his age with whom one can talk at length about nearly any
subject. When my mother died, in 1989, his was one of the most
memorable letters of condolence. He said that she was 'most reliable
in an emergency,' the highest praise; though I couldn't think to what
emergency he referred.
PATRICK GUINNESS (1980)

The last time that I saw Dr McDowell was in February 2000 – or was
it 1999 – in the Breakfast Room at the Kildare and University Club,
where I was staying at the time. He had stayed with us in Halifax and
I could not get over the detailed memories he still had of that visit,
details of which I had totally forgotten. Dr McDowell always was,
and no doubt still is, not only 'a scholar and a gentleman', to use an

old Irish compliment, but, perhaps even more rare, a wise man to boot, and we both wish him a very happy 90th birthday and many more of them.

JIM O'BRIEN & HEATHER O'BRIEN (LASKY) (1961)

During the Quartercentenary I was privileged to dine with Brendan McDowell at the Quo Vadis, and I was delighted to see that he had not changed in essentials. He had aged, of course, but nowhere near as much as we had. His conversation was as lively and captivating as ever. It was the highlight of my week in Dublin, after several decades' absence. Now that he is entering his 91st year, I am convinced that he is a permanent landmark, certainly so in the affections of JOSE XUEREB (1963)

The Emergency Speaker, Professor RB McDowell at the TCD Association dinner, 2000.

Speech and Speeches

The main thing that I remember was his high-pitched, rapid speech, which made it difficult to follow him at times. Someone commented that his brain was working so fast, his speech could never catch up! DR G. KEANE (1944)

I do wonder where RB got his amazing voice and accent – one could not mistake it in a crowd of a million! He can, on occasion, speak quite grandly, but there are always underlying Belfast/Dublin pronunciations. It's changed surprisingly little, over the years! His mother had a recognizable, but not strong, Belfast accent – what I've heard called a 'top-drawer Belfast accent'. There is a sort of conventional imitation of RB's voice that various people attempt, but no one ever gets it half right. It's quite unique. HENRY CLARK (1950)

But to enjoy him at his best and wittiest, one must listen to him in an after-dinner speech. There, our hero is on his mettle; his brain, which normally only works ten times as fast as that of an ordinary mortal, is now working twenty; his face is flushed, his eyes glittering; his hair awry, his spectacles askew, his hands gracefully scattering the wine glasses right and left and his boiled shirt heaving and buckling with the force of the tumultuous emotions in his breast beneath. And then, in that unforgettable voice, something between a neigh and a shriek, he begins! 'Well, of course ... ' TRINITY NEWS 22.5.58

I was in College long before RB became Junior Dean, but he was an eccentric lecturer and, when I first met him, in 1939, he was a character already and he took the chair at the Neophyte Debating Society, of which I was the last Secretary. The Society has long since expired – indeed, we had a banquet in my rooms in the Rubrics to mark the occasion – it was a sort of junior Hist but we were none of us orators, though capable of admiring RB McD's fantastic eloquence.
DR RICHARD McCLELLAND (1943)

He was seen to be an outstanding speaker from the first time that he attended one of our dinners up here, representing the Provost (TCD Graduates Association, North of England). He came up three more times and would have come up from London for our Centenary Dinner when he was eighty, had a chest infection not prevented it. I remember one of his classic ways to end a speech: 'A Speaker seeking a conclusion is like a drowning man looking for a raft. But when the drowning man cannot find a raft, he sinks. The Speaker unable to find a conclusion remains standing up!'
DR JOHN LEATHER (1952)

Billed as one of the speakers at some boring meeting in the GMB, he entertained us by listing all of the British Prime Ministers of the previous hundred years, with their religious affiliations.
EDGAR BRENNAN (1948)

Sometime in the winter of 1942 to 1943, McDowell came up to St Columba's College to give a lecture, one Saturday evening, to the Upper School on 'Some Aspects of Irish History'. He came to dinner in the Masters' Common Room at 7 o'clock and this was a pretty formal affair, with the Sub-Warden, Doctor Willis, at the head of the table. About eight other members of staff were also present, with McDowell sitting on the Sub-Warden's right. The College butler, Flood, kept an eye on proceedings. During dinner, somebody mentioned Waterford and, with that, McDowell was off! Only the previous week, he had travelled by train to Waterford and he proceeded to describe his journey south with such phrases as, 'the marvellous scenery', 'how suitable the Curragh was for army manoeuvres', 'the beautiful woods and pasture land' and remarked on what a magnificent city Kilkenny appeared to be. He talked at such length that Doctor Willis had to suggest to him that his meal would be getting cold and then came the revelation that, 'that was the first time I had been south of Dublin, I didn't really know that there was anything below Dublin, quite fascinating it was and the splendid river in Waterford, all very exciting,' and this was delivered to the whole table, in a very hurried tempo. We were all very amused and McD's lecture was a great success – several members of staff, who had been in to dinner, went along to the lecture and were enthralled by the lecturer's enthusiasm for his subject. NORMAN LUSH (1951)

It is rumoured that he exists on Dinners, that is, dinners to which he is invited as a speaker, and I have no reason to doubt this rumour. For he is a brilliant after-dinner orator and is constantly in demand in Dublin for post-prandial entertainment. His train of thought is sometimes difficult to follow; that's an understatement, it's often impossible. Nevertheless, once accustomed to his various idiosyncrasies of speech, one is entranced by the fluent wit and wealth of knowledge. His presence is demanded by smart society hostesses and, although his dress is not always to match the occasion, his verbosity is. TRINITY NEWS 1.2.62

He spoke at the TCD Association dinner three years ago. I saw him walking around St Stephen's Green muttering to himself on the afternoon of the lecture and I thought that there was no way that he could speak, but he spoke well, remembering people such as Oliver St John Gogarty. McDowell's speech was excellent and he asked me after his speech if it was okay, which struck me as being quite humble. RONALD N.G. FERGUSON (1972)

With the passing years, my memories of the JD have faded, to an extent that I cannot provide you with a favourite story. My most recent recollection is from the TCD Association Annual dinner in Dublin, in 1999 (I think it was 1999!), when he stood in as guest

Dr RB McDowell, speaker, with Terence Brady who proposed the vote of thanks at the London Dining Club, 13 February 2003.
PHOTO: ROB VAN MESDAG

Dr RB McDowell, speaker, with John Pearson, Chairman of the London Dining Club, 13 February 2003.
PHOTO: ROB VAN MESDAG

speaker at short notice, Mary Robinson being unable to attend. His opening remarks were most amusing, concerning the role and duties of the 'substitute' speaker, but I am afraid that you will have to see if anyone else can recall his exact words.
ADRIAN MORAN (1967)

My wife, Lesley (Love), and I were to attend a TCD Association dinner with President Mary Robinson as guest speaker and were very much looking forward to an enjoyable evening and an excellent after-dinner address. The speaker had to withdraw because of her move to the United Nations and we were asked if we would like a refund. We had made our plans and attended the dinner and to our delight the ex-Junior Dean had agreed to step in as guest speaker. He entertained the assembled company for thirty-five to forty minutes, with anecdotes and stories interspersed with many serious observations, in one of the finest after-dinner speeches that either of us have ever heard. RB McDowell on that occasion was not substitute speaker – as usual he excelled and just think what he could have done for the United Nations refugees! COURTENAY THOMPSON (1966)

At the height of his TV fame, in the early sixties, RB was asked to open the new HQ of, I think, the Irish Builders Association, in Leeson Street, or thereabouts. As a post-graduate student, I attended, no doubt lured by the prospect of free hospitality. In his characteristically excited and rapid-fire remarks, our hero concluded by admitting that he had thus far never opened anything in his life. 'Except our mouth!' interjected a member of his audience, to general appreciation.
PROFESSOR DAVID HARKNESS OBE (1967)

Once, he was being entertained in the Trocadero and was relating some stories about eighteenth-century Ireland. Something fell under the table. In looking for it McD continued his story, from under the table. He was under the table for a long time but never missed a beat in his delivery. RONALD N.G. FERGUSON (1972)

In or around 1998 Dr McDowell spoke, by invitation, to the Association at the Anchor Inn, Bankside, on TCD in his undergraduate days. He spoke to us for over an hour without notes and created a comprehensive and vivid picture of a time that to most of his hearers would have been a dimly remembered, or, indeed, historical era. The applause which followed his discourse was, fittingly, preceded by a brief and admiring silence. JOHN KEETCH (1968)

As a relatively well-behaved student, at the far end of College, I knew Dr McDowell by sight as JD, but not personally. However, I do recall the following part of a speech, which Dr McDowell gave to the Dublin University Sailing Club at its annual dinner, where he was guest speaker, sometime between 1960 and 1966. He said that he had two sailing stories, but that he was only going to tell us one, just in case he was invited a second time. He had been taken out in a row-ing-boat and it began to get rather rough and, as he thought, danger-ous. Simultaneously, he realized two things. Firstly, he was shortly going to meet his maker and, secondly, he was about to be sick. It sur-prised and concerned him that he was much more apprehensive about the second eventuality, than the first. JOHN HARWOOD (1963)

Dr McD stayed with us here in Halifax [Canada] for a couple of days, some time in the mid eighties. He'd come to the city to speak at a con-ference on Irish history at St Mary's University. On the day of his talk, I came downstairs to get his breakfast at the requested hour, and was walking past the bathroom next to his bedroom when I heard lots of sounds of splash and talk. Something on these lines: ... splosh, splash ...'In 1742, the situation ...' splosh splash ... 'And FitzGerald (or whoever) was to be found ...' splash splosh. (I can do it better in per-son.) What he was doing was rehearsing his speech, obviously with lots of gesticulation. One could fill in the bits of what he was saying by lifting something from one of his books.

Unfortunately – or maybe fortunately – when he was giving his talk, they had him stand in front of a lectern and as he finished read-ing the pages, he was dropping them on the floor; there must have been a bit of a breeze, because they were wafting around and some of the audience (myself included) became transfixed on these floating papers, waiting for the next one to fall. Naturally, there was some choked laughter from the audience each time the next piece fell, but he eventually noticed this and he must have realized what was taking people's attention away and stopped dropping them.

HEATHER O'BRIEN (LASKY) (1961)

When I was Secretary of the Knights of the Campanile, we invited him to our dinner, simply as a guest, not as a speaker. Proceedings completed, including speeches and someone bold asked the Junior Dean if he had any words to add. He stood and delivered an erudite and witty speech, wholly appropriate to the dinner and all without notes. Afterwards he explained that he never attended a function without giving some thought as to what he might say if he were asked to speak. Suffice it to say, I have followed his advice and on occasion it has stood me in very good stead.

STEPHEN RICHARDSON (1972)

RB was most helpful throughout my term as Junior Dean. Each Trinity Monday, he spoke to the new Scholars wittily and wisely, on the role of Scholarship in College. One year, when I thanked him for a very fine lecture, RB replied, 'Not at all, Barrett. Nowadays, I find it far easier to give a lecture than to listen to one!'

DR SEAN BARRETT (JUNIOR DEAN 1986-2000)

DR McDOWELL'S SPEECH TO THE LONDON DINING
CLUB, LONDON, 13 FEBRUARY 2003

*D*r *McDowell began by citing the three subjects on which he felt most qualified to speak. These are: Trinity, eighteenth-century Irish History – on which subject he is an authority – and himself! Choosing – to applause – to talk about himself, he remarked that he appears to have been chosen by Alumni to symbolize their time in College; a time when all were young, without responsibilities and when it could be said that things were generally going rather well. He felt, however, that the Campanile would have been an equally suitable choice, having certain additional advantages such as permanence and a bell that you can ring.*

[139]

Back row: Frank Mitchell, unknown.
Front row: Erskine Childers, Professor T.M. Moody, Gerald Giltrap and Dr RB McDowell, after a meeting of the History Society, *c.* 1948.

Recalling his duties as Junior Dean, Dr McDowell remarked that people seemed to think that he had been a sort of 'Sheriff of the Wild West', involved only with discipline, whereas in fact his duties had more closely resembled those of a hotel manager, dealing with matters of accommodation and administration.

His sparkling oration, flawlessly delivered, without either microphone or notes, held the audience spellbound. It was greeted with rapturous applause and a standing ovation. It was a stunning performance. A.L. (More, on page 40.)

Dr McDowell thought that the reason for the huge turnout was because he was a symbol of nostalgia for the Golden Era (1945 through to the 1970s), when Trinity was large enough to be a university, but small enough to be a college and there was a great *joie de vivre*, combined with intellectual hard work. ERIC LOWRY (1965)

I was invited – and most honoured to be so – to propose a vote of thanks to Dr McDowell, for the speech that he gave to the London Dining Club, in February 2003. Arriving at the Club on the appointed evening, I was told that Dr McDowell would like to see me before dinner. I found him sitting on a chair outside the bar, barely able to talk in anything other than a prolonged whisper, it seemed – the after-effects, apparently, of the severe chest infection that he had recently suffered. We sat next to each other at dinner and, having instructed him not to talk to me at all costs, in order to save what was left of his voice, after a couple of glasses of wine, he found himself unable to resist a good gossip and so we happily whispered to each other all through the dinner, a long conversation which served to remind me of the incredible range of subjects about which my Professor could talk, with an astounding depth of knowledge. But still, I feared for his voice, particularly since there was no microphone available to broadcast his speech, over a packed and typically vocal dining-room. Not that he would have used it, as he told me he that hated the contraption and had never had time for them anyhow or way.

Finally he was introduced and he was up on his feet. He was up on his feet, not like any other ninety-year-old, but like a greyhound

Scene in the debating hall (GMB) at Trinity College, Dublin, at the honorary members' debate, 20 June 1951. Dr RB McDowell rising on a point of order.

slipped from the traps. He was up on his feet, poised – or, might I say, posed – ready to talk the way that I remember seeing him, week in week out at lectures, all those years ago, one hand akimbo, chin tilted upwards, eyes widened and bright and perhaps deep in one pocket the other hand clutching a large bunch of keys. But, best of all – and perhaps even miraculously so – the voice that had been nothing but an all-but-inaudible undertone was suddenly restored to a bell-like clarity. Maybe the bell was not as loud and as strong as before, but the sound was wonderfully lucid – poetic, even – and it floated over the packed dining-room the way a flute played exquisitely can be heard for miles, even when played pianissimo. I doubt very much that anyone – even those who had crowded in at the back of the hall – missed a note – I mean, a word.

Not that he spoke with notes, as such – not even a scribbled outline lay on the table in front of him as a guide. He spoke *ex tempore* and he spoke with such brilliance, wit and understanding that it was, well … simply breathtaking. It was a performance – and, believe you me, performance is absolutely the right word – of such a staggering intellectual and humorous virtuosity, that he more than fully deserved (if that's possible) the standing ovation that he received, just as he merited the spontaneous rendition of 'For He's a Jolly Good Fellow', that followed instantly.

He sat down, cocked his wise old head round at me and smiled. Over to you, said the look. 'Well,' I began, when I'd got some of my breath back, 'as they say in variety – follow that.' And I meant it. I've followed some hard acts – but that was without doubt the toughest.

TERENCE BRADY (1961)

RB, after he had coxed the Staff IV to victory at Trinity Regatta in 1952. His crew carry him forward for the traditional cox's ducking. Photo copyright John Pearson.

The Hist and The Boat Club

THE HIST

In my days in College he was a dominant personality – I never got to know him very well, but he was an avid supporter of the 'Hist' and I well remember him musing about the excessive vulgarity of some of the songs which used to be sung by members, when in their cups after one of the Society dinners.

I enclose a photograph of him speaking at one of the CHS debates. I cannot remember the subject, or what was said, but McDowell's contribution was sure to have been witty and pertinent and probably devastating to the arguments of the other side! I am there on the left in the back row in a dinner jacket and wearing what appears to be a candidate bachelor's gown, which would place it in the summer of 1951. The man on the left in a white tie is H.R.F. Keating and Jim Kilfedder is sitting on the right of the chair. (We used to call Jim 'Shamus', probably to tease him about his Unionist proclivities – those were the days when Orange and Green happily rubbed shoulders in Trinity.) PETER LOFTUS (1951)

This is a story, I know is true because I was there. We had a debate in Trinity about Northern Ireland. Several well-known politicians came to speak, including Bernadette Devlin, as she then was. She arrived late, but spoke very passionately. Professor McDowell was on the opposite debating team and the theme of his speech was, that if you stood in Belfast, the differences between Catholic and Protestant look very great, but if you looked from Dublin, the differences between a Catholic and a Protestant looked smaller, from London smaller still, from New York hardly noticeable and from Tokyo these two groups looked like the same people. As he argued that everyone in Northern Ireland needed to put things into perspective, Bernadette got very upset and interrupted the Professor. My memory could not do justice to his eloquent quashing of her interruptions, but he managed to have the whole hall laugh at her, as though she was a silly teenager. She was furious. The Professor won the day by a large margin.

SAM DARBY (1975)

THE BOAT CLUB

Sometime, in the Hilary term of 1952, the Boat Club decided to have an event for the other clubs with a Fours race at Trinity Regatta. We also suggested that a lecturers' Four should be assembled and we approached several of the younger members of staff to find enthusiasts for the idea. Professor McDowell was already a favourite in the Boat Club, so there was no better choice for the cox of this Four. A number of practice outings were arranged and in the following term, Trinity Regatta was held, as usual, at Islandbridge, on the Friday and Saturday of Trinity Week. The River Liffey is only wide enough along the weir at Islandbridge for two boats to race side by side, so the lecturers had to win one, or possibly two, heats before entry to the final on the Saturday. Under the expert and challenging steering of Professor McDowell, the lecturers came in first to win the final to great acclaim from all those assembled on the bank. As winning cox, RB was thrown into the water.

That evening at Commons, there were, as usual, two Boat Club tables and for some reason Professor McDowell was slightly late and, therefore, the Dining Hall was fully assembled by the time of his arrival. As the cox of the lecturers' Four made his way up the centre aisle, at a pre-arranged signal, the two Boat Club tables rose as one man and began to applaud. The rest of the students, presumably without knowing what it was all about, also got to their feet and began to applaud, too. No doubt some explanation was required from the Professor to his colleagues. A somewhat shaken Scholar eventually took his place to say the familiar Latin Grace. It was, doubtless, a moment that Professor McDowell and everyone else will remember.

SIR WILLIAM DOUGHTY (1953)

Dr McDowell was always a very loyal supporter of the Boat Club, attending many of our functions as the witty speaker he always was and coxing a Club IV at Trinity Regatta most years. He still continues to enliven Lady Elizabeth Boat Club parties in London. He stays with LEBC members – Rob van Mesdag (late 1940s and early 1950s), John Pearson (mid 1950s) and Simon Newman (late 1950s and early 1960s) – for a few nights on a regular basis each year.

GERRY BLANCHARD (1965)

Nocturnal Rambles

RB McDOWELL REMEMBERS:

After conversations in the Common Room after Commons, I would go to the Library and/or the Junior Dean's office, where there was a typewriter, etc. I had the books on the stocks and lectures to prepare, so I would stay in the Library or JD office until 10 p.m., with a break at 9 p.m., when I would go over to my rooms to meet the porter, who would conduct me to Night Roll. Of course, on a number of evenings I would have an engagement, social or academic, in or out of College. Thus, I was rarely in my rooms except when I was a host.

I went up to Trinity in 1946 and got to know RB quite early in my first year. Thereafter, we saw each other very regularly. I remember particularly long late-night walks through Dublin, for example, to Henrietta Street, once the smartest Georgian address in Dublin, reserved for peers alone and in the 1940s – and probably still – a slum. Also, trips on Sunday afternoons into the Wicklows and to Enniskerry, etc. where he used to call on friends.

HENRY CLARK (1950)

As a voluntary fire warden at TCD, during 1941, I was escorted, one night, by RB McDowell. He spent the night pointing out the unmarked graves of various College worthies, with a non-stop account

of their lives and achievements. Not sure if it helped the fire-fighting exercise, but it was much better fun!
PROFESSOR MAURICE JASWON (1944)

I was there before the time of RB being Junior Dean, but no doubt everyone will be inundated with stories of him during this time and many, too, of him suddenly appearing in an apparently empty Nassau Street at 2 a.m., twiddling his keys, having materialized through the 'invisible' gate from the Fellows' Garden.
DR JOHN LEATHER (1952)

One funny story about RB, which he occasionally relates, is about his keys. He used to have the keys of the private gate from Nassau Street into the Trinity Fellows' Garden, as a short cut from the Club. The keys were tied to a short stick and RB had a nervous habit of swinging the keys on their string, round and round. I knew it well. Then, one night, just as he got into the garden, the string broke and the keys flew off into the bushes. I'd like to say that I was with him, but it was someone else who told me of a frantic search, until the keys were found amid many of RB's exclamations of, 'Oh, my goodness!' and an occasional, 'My God!' HENRY CLARK (1950)

I have a vague memory of somebody emptying their tub of water out of the window in rooms and it disastrously going over McDowell as he made his evening rounds.
DAVID FRANKLIN (1953)

At a party, the JD was talking to us about noises in the night: 'It's very disturbing if the man in the rooms above you sits down on the bed and takes off his shoes, dropping one onto the floor. You are kept awake waiting for him to drop the other. Also, it's disturbing to be woken up when one of your books falls off your bed onto the floor.'
CANON PETER NORTON (1961)

There was something of the night about McDowell!
DAVID GILLIAT (1961)

On a winter's night in the 1970s a carpet of snow-covered Front Square. After Commons, I finished my coffee and left the Common Room a few minutes after McDowell. As I stepped out into the snow-storm, I was alarmed to see a sinister shape, apparently human, prone on the cobblestones. Alongside the GMB there appeared a shadowy but familiar figure wearing an unmistakable hat and coat, quite clear-ly making a search. On reaching Front Square, the figure plucked the MA gown from its resting-place and set off rapidly towards No. 24.

DR R.A. SOMERVILLE (1972), Dept of Economics, TCD

My only close encounters of the curious kind with the JD occurred one evening in College Park, as my final exams approached. I'd been reading and drinking black coffee all day, in No. 30, so I thought that I'd get some fresh air before turning in. I strolled at a leisurely pace to begin with. There was nobody about and it was pretty dark. Then I heard footsteps behind me, so I quickened my stride, more and more as the footsteps behind me grew faster and faster. Finally, I was all but running, when a hand clutched my sleeve. It was the JD, puffing. 'I only wanted to say hello!' he gasped.

DAVID MARIANO (1962)

I have vivid memories, after fifty years or so, of taking long walks with him round and round College Park, at midnight and after. We discussed, or rather he discussed and I chipped in from time to time, the curiosities of human behaviour and history, both in the abstract and the particular and the story of the College as he remembered it and had inquired into it.

But, after the long lapse of time I cannot recall, word for word, anything he said and you can imagine how much, in the course of a long half-hour or a short hour, he was able to say. But I can state with assurance, that of all that I learned at TCD in the years 1948 to 1952, those conversations, one-sided as they may have been, formed a con-siderable part.

H.R.F. KEATING (1952)

Chance Encounters

I recall bumping into him by chance in Fleet Street, in the 1980s, when I worked in the City and talking briefly about the financial markets. An adjacent hoarding had Ulster loyalist fly-posters on it, reading, 'Ulster says No', which I pointed out to him. A wag had written under one: '... but the man from Del Monte says "Yes".' I had to explain what that meant. PATRICK GUINNESS (1980)

I recall him as a junior, and already somewhat eccentric, History lecturer – I think he succeeded ERR Green, *c.* 1945. As is well-known, his appearance scarcely changed over fifty years – the hat, the scarf, etc. In the seventies and eighties, I used to see him occasionally scurry amid the precincts of the University of London Senate House during vacations – no doubt at the Institute of Historical Research.
ERIC EARLE (1947)

I had been invited by Felicity Roche, together with my wife, Susi, to spend the weekend of 10/11 October, 1992, in the famous Pen-y-Gwyrd Hotel, in Snowdonia, to take part in a surprise party in honour of her husband, Professor Laurence Roche, who was retiring from the Chair of Forestry at the University of Bangor in North Wales. The first guest I saw at the hotel was Professor RB McDowell, while, gradually, others with TCD associations began to foregather. The evening was a memorable success. RB McDowell gave a splendidly witty speech; I inflicted my happy mixture of verse and prose in honour of Laurence and Felicity on the gathering and so, in due course, to bed.

The following morning at breakfast, I was in high company, with Professors McDowell and Trevor West, discussing possible alcoholic killings to be had in the Duty Free sector of the ferry. McDowell told West and myself that he never bought drink at Duty Free, because of the danger of a bottle breaking. Ignoring the warnings, I bought a litre bottle of Powers Gold Label Whiskey (for £10) and two modest bottles of Bulgarian wine (for £1.95 per bottle). Shortly before disembarkation, our bottle bags fell over, knocking against the leg of a chair, with a distinct sound of glass meeting glass. Only too soon, the smell of whiskey pervaded our area and McDowell had proved himself to be a prophet newly inspired. When I next met him, no doubt in Front Square, I regaled him with the story of my loss of £10, which justified his attitude towards bottles in Duty Free.

MORGAN DOCKRELL (1960)

During the long vacation, a senior colleague (sadly I cannot remember who) was ascending on an escalator in the London Underground, when he observed RB McDowell descending on the adjacent escalator. There were delighted greetings and RB, forgetting the situation, enthusiastically started to explain his latest research findings, as he descended into the depths! (This story was told to me by the late David Webb. Who was on the upward escalator sadly I have forgotten, but their personality added to the amusement I remember.) Maybe somebody else knows this story?

DR I.K. FERGUSON OBE (1964)

I met him only once after I left Dublin. It was on a Tube train somewhere in West London. Suddenly, I realized an altogether familiar figure was sitting a few yards away. I hailed him. He came over, in his dark overcoat, to where my wife was sitting with our two-year-old son. He raised his hat to her, with the nervous gesture I remembered. He gave a guarded glance at boisterous, wriggling Simon. We talked for a few minutes. Then our station came up.

H.R.F. KEATING (1952)

I met him in the Blue Post Pub at the London Association AGM, in December 2000. He had travelled by Underground from his London 'pied à terre' and I thought him very brave. Travelling by London Transport is such a battle. I am always amazed that, after fifty years, he looks exactly the same and seems to be wearing the same clothes – hat and scarf – as when we were in College. When you meet him it's a comfort. The world has stood still. DR RUTH BLACKALL (1957)

Jackie and I met him a year or two back, at a party given by one of our neighbours who was doing historical research at King's College, I believe, and had the temerity to sit in 'his' seat. They then became bosom chums. He seemed to be exactly the same as I remember him and Jackie noted, rather unkindly, that he was obviously wearing the same cardigan as when we were at University!
PATRICK KEITH CAMERON (1961)

My own memories of Dr McDowell date from after my time in College, although I was of course 'aware of his presence' as Junior Dean, as was every undergraduate of my vintage – the mid-60s. I remember, however, seeing Dr McDowell one hot summer day in the late seventies or early eighties walking briskly along Piccadilly, wearing, I suspect, the same overcoat, hat and scarf as he had been accustomed to wear around TCD in the mid sixties. JOHN KEETCH (1968)

He had an excellent memory, I had attended his lectures as a, not particularly outstanding, student. I visited Trinity after some years and saw him approaching me in College Park. He did not look up as he passed, but I heard him mutter amongst all the mass of his vocalized thoughts, 'There goes Lacy!' STERLING LACY (1973)

He is so used to being the centre of attention; recently I saw him processing out of the Dining Hall acknowledging the crowd like a visiting Potentate!
PAULINE MILLINGTON-WARD (GOODBODY) (1961)

Despite the apparent vagueness, two years after leaving Trinity, my girlfriend, now wife, and I were crossing the Cromwell Road in London and met him on a traffic island, where he addressed me by name. Impressive. ROGER KYNASTON (1966)

He certainly did have, and maybe still has, an astonishing memory. At one time, I found some old books in a family house in County Cork and took them to him, to see if he would either give me, or get somebody else to give me, some idea of their value. I went to Canada and forgot about them for several years. A good five years plus later, I was back in Dublin and one day remembered that I had left these books with him. On the off-chance that he might still have them or know who did, I went to see him in his wonderfully untidy (at least to everyone but himself) rooms. Without a moment's hesitation, he went to a pile of books on the floor and at once picked up mine from the pile. He knew exactly where they were, after all that time.
JIM O'BRIEN (1961)

Another story concerning the JD took place fifteen or more years ago. John Spearman, graduate of TCD and businessman, was sitting in his luxurious limousine in heavy traffic in Gower Street, London, making a business telephone call. Before he was aware of what was happening, the JD, who had been walking along nearby, leapt into the car and settled himself in. 'Oooooh, Spearman, how very convenient,' he said. 'Ludgate Circus, please!' DOUGLAS WRIGHT (1968)

I took my then twelve-year-old daughter to the London Library. She had never seen a million books before. We wandered around, picking up a book here and another book there. My daughter was acting as bearer. Suddenly, we turned a corner and there was RB McD! I effected an introduction – my daughter so loaded down with books that she had no hand to shake hands with. RB McD, thinking that the books were ones which she had chosen, examined the pile and proceeded to congratulate her, aged, as I say, twelve, on her choice. 'What's this? Oh, the memoirs of Alexander Herzen! An excellent choice, my dear.' To this day, my daughter asks if I ever see 'that nice gentleman' we met in the London Library.
ROBERT BAILEY-KING

Random Memories

Some time in the mid-forties McDowell and I were walking together down Grafton Street. He was discoursing, at the top of his voice, I need hardly say, on the topic of how our vocabulary and style is adjusted, to take account of the company we are in. 'For example,' he said, 'I would not use the word "bugger" in the presence of Dr Luce.' An elderly man toddling down the street a few yards in front of us turned round to look and was, of course, Dr A.A. Luce.
MAURICE CRAIG (1944)

Really our paths never crossed except perhaps in Front Square, when he was hurrying to somewhere else and his bent figure produced an imaginary 'bow wave', signalling, to me at least, 'Don't stop me!'
R. GRANT COLEMAN (1936)

Only the shy shade of the College Dean and the quality of the voice remain with me. RONALD PIGOTT (1954)

When I was in TCD, I lived in 18, Botany Bay, and shared these rooms with David Minch. One evening, RB knocked on the door and enquired if Minch was in. I replied, 'Sorry, I fear he is out.' He remarked, 'You don't sound too bright,' and I replied, 'Yes, I am recovering from 'flu.' One minute he was there and the next he was gone. A voice from way down the stairs called up, 'I've been trying to avoid it all winter!' DR CHRISTOPHER PETIT (1956)

My memory is related to my first week in College. A very shy, uncertain Fresher, I plucked up courage and ventured for the first time into the Reading Room. It seemed the only available seat was conveniently at the table nearest the door and desk, so I sat there, complete with virgin reading list and notebook. While I waited for my first request to arrive, I was aware of what I can only describe as 'heavy breathing' behind me and I could feel a presence hovering. On looking around, I found this rather distinctive and slightly surprising figure (I had never seen such a long scarf) standing scratching his forehead and clearly thinking that a cuckoo had occupied a favourite seat. I had no idea who he was or whether this was an unofficially reserved seat left vacant for him, so I picked up my belongings and fled. Not that he said anything or complained, but I just felt as if I had done the wrong thing and never again attempted to sit downstairs. Come to think of it, I never did discover if it was an unspoken rule that that seat should be left free. WENDY WILKINSON (1955)

A Junior Freshman friend was in the Reading Room attempting to study, when a man sat next to him restlessly and noisily turning the pages of his book, as well as loudly muttering to himself. My friend eventually said, 'Do you mind keeping quiet?' The man looked up and said, 'Oh, I am so sorry!' The man was, of course, the Junior Dean. STERLING LACY (1973)

The JD was talking after the blowing-up of Nelson's monument in O'Connell Street. This was after I left TCD. 'At first, I thought it was a drunken student falling downstairs, but the noise did not continue, so I knew it was something different,' said the JD.
CANON PETER NORTON (1961)

From Desmond Tyndall, the present Bluebottle: 'A colleague told McDowell he should get married. McDowell's reply was, "I suppose I should. But I'd need to marry some capable, formidable woman-eh, I suppose, somebody like the matron of the Adelaide."'
DR W.E. VAUGHAN, Dept of Modern History, TCD

When I edited the *Trinity Trust News*, I asked McDowell to write something anecdotal about the Junior Dean – the office and its holders. Eventually, we arranged to meet after Commons, in order for me to write while McDowell dictated. You may imagine my difficulty in keeping up, as I do not have shorthand. However, another difficulty emerged: you will know that McDowell is a man of immense discretion and consequently many of his best anecdotes finished with the injunction: 'Of course, you couldn't possibly print that.'
DR R.A. SOMERVILLE (1972) Dept of Economics, TCD

For reasons I've never understood, I was appointed Junior Dean in the 1970s. Dr McDowell, a superb former Junior Dean, said I would do the job well. 'Well, Brendan,' he said, 'You know every rule there is to know. After all, you broke most of them as an undergraduate.'
PROFESSOR BRENDAN KENNELLY (1961), School of English, TCD. Junior Dean, 1969–1971.

After leaving Trinity, I spent a year in Paris at L'Ecole du Louvre and then returned to College to do an M. Litt. in Irish History. I approached Professor McDowell and he kindly agreed to supervise my thesis. I knew him socially, as well as at TCD. As my supervisor, he sometimes took me to tea at the University Club and I remember, on one occasion, he left me alone in a small room. Shortly afterwards, a Church of Ireland clergyman put his head round the door, looked at me and left. Then another Protestant cleric arrived and did the same thing. The next person wore gaiters – presumably, a Bishop! The Bishop also stared and then withdrew just as quickly as his predecessors. Dr McDowell returned shortly afterwards and it was only as we were leaving the room that I saw a large sign on the door marked, very clearly, '*Clergy Only*'. I felt that they might have been even more disturbed had they known, not only was the intruder a female, but a Holy Roman, to boot! BRIDGET HULL (1961)

David Greene was a great friend of McDowell. He was a big man with a big beard who wore a big shapeless suit and was famed far and wide for his willingness to sit up all night, talking and being convivial. One day, in the 1980s, he and RB were walking together through College Park, when McDowell was heard to remark, 'It's a great pity there are no characters left in Trinity!'

DR RAYMOND REES (1944)

Felicitous Phrases

I heard him say, 'Excessive verbosity can become a trifle overbearing!'
Of all the people! DR JOHN LEATHER (1952)

Sir Robert Tate said, 'McDowell talks a lot but he talks sense.'
JOHN PEARSON (1956)

Out in the country for a walk one day, suddenly he realised that time
had passed and he had an engagement. He also realised that he had
no money, so he knocked on a door and asked for a loan (to pay his
fare), saying that he was *suffering from a temporary pecuniary
embarrassment*. I don't know how he managed to pronounce that,
with his customary speed of speaking. KATE TIMMS (1952)

Once, in recent years, I was strolling along, eating some chocolate,
when I met RB. I offered him some of the chocolate. He graciously
declined, saying, 'I must admit that, though I consider it unseemly to
eat chocolate in public, it is one of the delights of solitude.'
PROFESSOR BRENDAN KENNELLY (1961)

'Yes, I am in my anecdotage.' Reply by RB to my thanks for his witty
anecdotes in an address to the new Scholars on Trinity Monday afternoon.
DR SEAN BARRETT, Dept of Economics, TCD

Of all the machinery of the IT world, he said recently: 'I simply adore
these machines. They improve my conversational powers. They simply force me to talk more!'
PROFESSOR BRENDAN KENNELLY (1961)

God! Is he ninety? Not another dozen birthday parties! ANON.

I used to talk an awful lot when I was young. RB McD

People are very unreliable when it comes to repeating a story.
RB McD

How do you cope with ladies walking past? One didn't want to be
rude! RB McD

In the Reading Room: 'I am a great believer in waiting one's turn, so
long as the queue is not too long!' RB McD

I was thinking of what I was saying, which is always rather fatal.
RB McD

I remember my tutor saying, 'McDowell, I always thought you were
a gentleman – until I heard you translating Virgil!' RB McD

On reading these contributions by Alumni:
'I'd better not go on reading – I'll get too self-satisfied!'
DR RB McDOWELL

The Last Word

'RB'

     'RBD'

         'McD'

           'RBMcD'

              'Dr McD'

          'Dr McDowell'

       'Professor McDowell'

     'The Prof'

'McDowell'

     'The Junior Dean'

       'The Incredible Man'

         'The White Rabbit'

           'The Great Man'

'The Caped Character of Front Square'

but, to the Alumni of TCD,
he will always be, affectionately, just

'THE JD!'

Glossary

Auditor	President of the Hist (College debating society).
Botany Bay	One of three spacious squares, containing accommodation units known as 'Rooms.' So called, because it originally contained a herb garden.
Commencements	Ceremony for conferring degrees.
Commons	Ceremonial meal served in the eighteenth century Dining Hall, a tradition that has existed almost since the foundation of the College.
The Junior Dean	College officer responsible for accommodation in College and for enforcing discipline.
Knights of the Campanile	Established in 1926 to entertain visiting Oxford and Cambridge teams. Their tie is pink for Trinity, dark blue for Oxford and light blue for Cambridge.

Library	One of only six copyright libraries in the British Isles. The Library's right to claim a copy of all books and periodicals, maps and sheet music published in the UK and Ireland is enshrined by charter in both countries.
Little-Go	Examination for Honours students at the end of their Senior Freshman year. Arts undergraduates took two scientific subjects and science undergraduates, two arts subjects. Discontinued in 1969.
Long Room (of the Library)	Dates from 1732. Described as 'one of the most spectacular spaces in Ireland,' it is the oldest single chamber library in the world. Contains about 200,000 of the Library's oldest books, including the Book of Kells
Moderatorship	'Mod.' Honours degree. Four years to complete.
Pink	Awarded to outstanding sportsmen and women at national and international level. Pink was Elizabeth I's racing colour.
Players	Dublin University Players: the college amateur dramatic society, which had a theatre at No. 4, Front Square.
The Reading Room	Octagonal reading room built in 1937.

Rooms	450 sets of sitting-rooms and bed-rooms in College. Until 1972, available to male undergraduates only.
Schol	Academic distinction awarded to undergraduates who are known as 'Scholars' and become members of the body corporate of the College. These awards are announced by the Provost on Trinity Monday.
Second Grace	Grace after meat.
Sizar	Holder of a scholarship awarded on entry. Includes free Commons.
Skip	College domestic servant.
Trinity Monday	First day of 'Trinity Week' on which the Provost announces the names of new Fellows and Scholars.
Trinity Week	Takes place in June with a number of social and sporting events, culminating in the famous Trinity Ball.
'Wife'	Person sharing College rooms.
Junior Freshman	1st-year undergraduate
Senior Freshman	2nd-year undergraduate
Junior Sophister	3rd-year undergraduate
Senior Sophister	4th-year undergraduate
Michaelmas Term	Christmas Term
Hilary Term	Spring Term
Trinity Term	Summer Term

Index of Contributors